What We Hunger For

· · · · · · · · ·

What We Hunger For

. . . .

Refugee and Immigrant Stories about Food and Family

Edited by 신 선 영 *Sun Yung Shin*

MINNESOTA
HISTORICAL
SOCIETY PRESS

The publication of this book was supported by a generous grant from the Elmer L. and Eleanor Andersen Publications Fund and through a gift from an anonymous donor..

mnhspress.org

The Minnesota Historical Society Press is a member of the Association of University Presses.

Manufactured in the United States of America

10 9 8 7 6 5 4 3 2

♾

The paper used in this publication meets the minimum requirements of the American National Standard for Information Sciences—Permanence for Printed Library Materials, ANSI Z39.48-1984.

International Standard Book Number
ISBN: 978-1-68134-197-2 (paper)
ISBN: 978-1-68134-198-9 (e-book)

Library of Congress Control Number: 2021930049

This and other Minnesota Historical Society Press books are available from popular e-book vendors.

Contents

· · · · · · · · · · · · · · · ·

Introduction

· · · · · · · · · · · · · · · ·

신 선 영 *Sun Yung Shin*

The Pew Research Center reports, "The United States has more immigrants than any other country in the world. Today, more than 40 million people living in the U.S. were born in another country, accounting for about one-fifth of the world's migrants. The population of immigrants is also very diverse, with just about every country in the world represented among U.S. immigrants. . . . Since the creation of the federal Refugee Resettlement Program in 1980, about 3 million refugees [included in the above number of immigrants] have been resettled in the U.S.—more than any other country."[1]

I am one of those 40 million immigrants and refugees. I am not indigenous to this land; I am not a citizen of any of the sovereign nations of Native people on this land. I was born in Seoul, South Korea, and am an ethnic Korean of the diaspora. I continue to learn and receive teaching from Native writers, scholars, artists, colleagues, and friends about what it means to be a good relative, to be a good guest, and to fulfill my obligations to the first peoples. A writer who has had a direct influence on me and on the genesis of this book is the extraordinary Diane Wilson, a Dakota author whose essay "Seeds for Seven Generations" I chose for inclusion in *A Good Time for the Truth: Race in Minnesota* (2016), my first anthology with the Minnesota Historical Society Press.

---

[1] Abby Budiman, "Key Findings about US Immigrants," Pew Research Center, August 20, 2020, https://www.pewresearch.org/fact-tank/2020/08/20/key-findings-about-u-s-immigrants.

Espousing a philosophy of gratitude and reciprocity for the gifts of nature, Wilson's essay is last in that book because I believe that in order to survive and thrive on this warming planet, we need to be part of worldwide decolonization (or un-colonization) movements, including of our food systems. We need to make reciprocity with the earth a priority, and as Dr. Robin Wall Kimmerer, an enrolled member of the Citizen Potawatomi Nation and a plant ecologist, and others passionately advocate, we need to heal our broken relationship with the land. And we need to bring our children. The penultimate paragraph in Wilson's piece speaks to this brokenness, and the solution: "Today many of our children are growing up in paved cities, afraid of bees, unable to recognize plants, and often completely ignorant of where their food comes from. And yet they will inherit this world; they will become its stewards. We are responsible for teaching our children that plants and animals are co-creating this world with us, and the lessons they offer can help us reverse the harms that humans have inflicted. As we say in Dakota, Mitakuye Oyasin. We Are All Related."

Water and food are life and always have been. Many surnames in the English language indicate a food-related profession: Miller, Baker, Cook, Fisher, Shepherd, Skinner, Gardener, Cooper, Potter. Does your name, by any chance, have anything to do with food or flavor? My names have a complicated personal history, but I'd like to share something about them that I find delightful, and that has inspired me, in an unintended way, as I have put this book together.

In the Korean writing system, or Hangeul, my name is written as 신 선 영, Shin Sun Yung. In formal Chinese (called Hanja), my name is written as 辛善英. "Shin" or "Xin" can be written in different ways in Chinese. The way my surname, *Shin*, is written, 辛, means *pungent* or *spicy*. (In Korea, the family name comes first, as many people know.)

I have naturally taken this personal etymology as a good sign that I have some authority to shepherd a book about food, cooking, and eating into the world. I have loved spicy food for as long as I can remember, and generally the hotter the better, where the pain is just enough—but not too much—to turn into gustatory pleasure.

Contemplating my name led me to dig deeper into the meaning of *spicy*. It's not a flavor quality, not like sweet, salty, bitter, sour, and savory (often known as *umami* in the foodie world). I looked to science and happily found an abundance of information. Scientists have identified the cause of *spicy* as capsaicin, which is a chemical compound (8-methyl-N-vanillyl-6-nonenamide) found in chili peppers, first isolated in crystalline form in 1878. It causes a burning sensation in mucous membranes, *and* it is medicinal. According to the National Institutes of Health's National Library of Medicine, "Capsaicin is a chili pepper extract with analgesic properties. Capsaicin is a neuropeptide releasing agent selective for primary sensory peripheral neurons. Used topically, capsaicin aids in controlling peripheral nerve pain."[2] A substance that can both cause pain and relieve pain? A paradox of magic!

Speaking of magic, one of the great pleasures of reading and writing about food is learning and savoring the names of plants, the names of concoctions, of dishes, of methods and tools. Our stimulating friend the chili pepper gets its Anglicized name from the Nahuatl word *chīlli*, and although categorized as a vegetable in the American mainstream grocery store, a chili pepper is the fruit of plants from the genus Capsicum, which belong to Solanaceae, a nightshade family. (*Solanaceae*. Solar. Night. Shade. Poetry!) Others in this family are tobacco, potato, tomato, and eggplant, all of which contain the alkaloid saponin called solanine (a neurotoxin, which is indeed poisonous in very large doses).

---

[2] See "Capsaicin," PubChem, National Center for Biotechnology Information, National Library of Medicine, https://pubchem.ncbi.nlm.nih.gov/compound/Capsaicin.

Sadly, many of us today, compared to generations past, are often divorced from our food sources and estranged from nature in general. To write about food can be a way of investigating and fostering a deeper understanding of our place in the natural world and what our reciprocal relationships were, should, and could be. To understand how we eat and nourish ourselves and our communities is a way of apprehending our true interdependence, a kind of intimacy. The intimacy of all things. Land. Water. Air. Bodies. Birth. Living. Death. Rebirth.

But why this book? Why me and why now? It's true, I am not a professional chef or cook, recipe writer, food critic, or flavor inventor. I'm just a writer and cultural worker who loves to learn about foods on this amazing planet of ours, and who has been hungry for a collection of food essays by writers who are immigrants or refugees themselves or grew up in such families.

I'm a mother who has raised two children and has fed them thousands of meals. I'm a friend who has shared wonderful, memorable, pleasurable, and earthy meals—from the elaborate to the simple and everything in between—with dear ones over the decades in homes and in neighborhood restaurants all over this and a few other countries, including my homeland, Korea.

I'm a daughter who learned how to grow tiny wild strawberries in the edges of the backyard garden of our small white house in a working-class suburb southwest of Chicago, *and* how to use a meat tenderizer mallet on a tough cut of steak from my mother; how to flood the yard at night with the garden hose in order to lure out the earthworms to catch to use as fish bait, *and* how to clean and fillet prehistoric, black, shark-like catfish in the fish house from my father; and I'm a granddaughter who learned how to strip the thick papery husks and the soft shining silk from corn, *and* how to peel a bright green apple with a paring knife from my grandmother. These experiences are like gold to me.

Though we immigrants and refugees may come from thousands of years of culinary history and practices, as newcomers to the United States our perspectives and insights on how "America" grows, raises, hunts, fishes, butchers, dries, prepares, stores, bakes, roasts, smokes, distributes, shops, cooks, remixes, invents, shares, receives, and eats is underrepresented in mainstream media. Too often our spice combinations, flavor palettes, visual symbols and aesthetics, and traditions are appropriated without credit or care by restaurateurs, recipe writers, and so on.

In my writing career I've always tried to work what could be called cross-culturally rather than mono-ethnically, for the most part, because my own life has been such a combination of traditions, lineages, foods, and stories, and I want to bring people together to understand each other better, especially those of us whose stories are underrepresented yet often appropriated.

The plot twist in my own gustatory journey is, briefly, that I was born a citizen of South Korea, underwent a separation from my family, and became a citizen of the United States at the age of five after being adopted by a white family in Chicago. I've been back to the Korean peninsula five times so far, and it's been a central part of my path to understanding my place in the world, including the world of plants, nonhuman animals, and cooking. My adoptive family, especially my mother, encouraged the tastes with which I arrived, and she never teased me about my pungent kimchi in the family refrigerator.

While my American mom didn't teach me Korean cooking herself, she gave me a solid foundation of kitchen fundamentals, including gardening and baking, that continue to serve me as I grow as a savorer and recipe-attempter of many global food traditions, including that of my homeland. I love Korean food: its emphasis on fruits, vegetables, and roots, its unique sweet and sour flavors, its art of fermentation, and its overall earthiness.

I became a vegetarian at the age of sixteen when I read an article somewhere about how cattle farming was contributing to the rapid destruction of the Amazon forest. I'm in my forties now, and I've remained a vegetarian, and occasionally delved into veganism. Although I don't eat meat, most of my friends and family do, and I respect their traditions and tastes. As we as a species continue to adapt to human-caused climate change, I hope we will examine all of our food systems, invest in preservation and revitalization of indigenous foodways, fight for community autonomy of growers and food producers, and apply a justice lens to all parts of our culture, including how we can live in reciprocal, respectful, and learning relationships with all land and with all fellow forms of life on this planet.

This book is so full of life, so vibrant, and so juicy. I am excited to share these essays with you. These writers have mined their multilayered, multisensory memories for you; they have brought their best storytelling gifts to these pages about food and families. You will find poetics of food both collective and idiosyncratic. You will travel to fragrant places here and there. You will see the beautifully human complexities in each author through their multifaceted relationships to food and family.

There is every human emotion here, and hard truths fought for and won, in private and public scenes (and in between). There is unbearable loss, grief, and anguish. There are intergenerational chasms for many of us that may not be bridged in this lifetime.

Some things, perhaps many, can never be recovered, and healing is never a given, especially for those of us living in a country that often sends us the message that we are not wanted, that we are a burden, a parasite, a problem. For many of us it is a daily struggle to be treated with dignity and to fulfill our potential. But for many of us, writing is healing, not because it makes things *okay* but because it allows us to work through our experiences, give shape to them, empower ourselves and each other by holding space for our stories and perspectives.

Pulitzer Prize–winning refugee writer Viet Thanh Nguyen wrote in an op-ed for the *New York Times* that what Asian Americans and underrepresented moviegoers and literature readers want, among other things, is something he's calling *narrative plenitude*:

> I came up with that idea in my book *Nothing Ever Dies: Vietnam and the Memory of War.* Narrative plenitude is what makes it possible for Hollywood to make so many Vietnam War movies. Not just *Apocalypse Now* and *The Deer Hunter* but also *Platoon* and *Full Metal Jacket* and *Rambo.* They are all set in Vietnam, and some of them are excellent works of art, but they are all dramas of white American masculinity. The Vietnamese are extras in these movies, who exist only to mutter, grunt, groan, curse and jabber incomprehensibly until they are rescued, raped or killed.
>
> But these are American movies, you might say. Of course they should be about Americans. That does not explain why blacks, Latinos, Native Americans, women or yes, Asian-Americans, all of whom served in the American military, barely appear in these movies.
>
> It matters because I, and most other Asian-Americans, grew up and still live in the opposite of "narrative plenitude." We live in an economy of narrative scarcity, in which we feel deprived and must fight to tell our own stories and fight against the stories that distort or erase us. Many Americans will take these Asian images—which are usually awful—and transfer them to any Asian-American they encounter.[3]

The fourteen talented writers collected here are contributing to the expanding narrative plenitude of food writing by writers of color in America. Some other writers, cooks, and chefs who have influenced my thinking for this book project include local

---

[3] Viet Thanh Nguyen, "Asian Americans Need More Movies, Even Mediocre Ones," *New York Times*, August 21, 2018.

luminaries Heid Erdrich and her book *Original Local: Indigenous Foods, Stories, and Recipes from the Upper Midwest;* Sean Sherman and his book *The Sioux Chef's Indigenous Kitchen,* co-written with Beth Dooley; Rose McGee and her Sweet Potato Comfort Pie project; and writers and cooks in other regions such as Michael W. Twitty and his book *The Cooking Gene: A Journey Through African American Culinary History in the Old South;* Korean monk Jeong Kwan, featured in *Chef's Table* season three; Samin Nosrat and her book *Salt, Fat, Acid, Heat;* Bryant Terry and his book *Afro-Vegan: Farm-Fresh African, Caribbean, and Southern Flavors Remixed;* Padma Lakshmi and her show *Taste the Nation;* David Chang and his show *Ugly Delicious;* and many others changing the conversation nationally and internationally about who and what is valuable and worthy of attention. I learn about the dazzling variety of practitioners everywhere, every day, by exploring social media, reviews, and bookshelves and letting, with great pleasure and curiosity, one great cook or food writer lead me to another and another.

It is my hope that you will travel through these essays with us in the spirit of narrative plenitude, in appreciation of all the things that have to come together in this world for us to satisfy our hunger for food, connection, and meaning. Enjoy!

Grandma's Portal

· · · · · · · · · · · · · · · ·

Ifrah Mansour

The art of canjeero starts with a secret
as ancient as the first Somali footprints,
on the longest, bluest African coastline,
endlessly kissing the Indian Ocean.
"Are we a love child from strange travelers,
or are we terribly un-tannable Africans
with silk hairs and soft-syllable names—a colonizer's favorite?"

Mispronounce namesakes,
injera or lahoh or somali pancakes.
Some eat it for breakfast.
Some serve it on a special occasion.
I devour it to keep my grandmother's memory alive.

Canjeero's ingredients are softly guarded
like the baby hairs on a baby girl
crying in a foreigner's language,
far away from her roots.
Canjeero is a refugee's sacred inheritance.

Canjeero is a recipe without borders,
a recipe orally memorized to feed Americanized generations.
Canjeero is the unsung heroes
for the first-generation immigrants raising leaders in the projects,
constantly stretching food stamps
to feed large families.
Canjeero is the love language of abundance.

Every canjeero is different,
like each monarch's journey to the south.
Yet the hunger for one's roots is as real
as the hunger in the refugee camps we once called home.
Canjeero is a remnant of an uncolonized indigenous cuisine.

The making of canjeero begins with an old prayer, said by a
    dark-skinned farmer, my ayeeyo.

Canjeero is a magical mixture of homemade sourdough starter,
all-purpose flour, cornmeal flour,
bit of sugar, pinch of salt,
and ample amounts of water.
Beat it before the midnight hour.
Let your hands *clap clap,*
singing praises to each
ounce of the dough.
Let the dough be liquidy like honey.
Let it be free of lumps like pudding.
Lid it like a living treasure safeguarding your spirit.

Let the dough rest at ease.
Let it meditate on the nameless pains inside of you.
Let love from the ancestors pour in and double the dough's size.

Let the morning light welcome your first canjeero.
Choose a cast-iron or regular pan;
heat it to a warm embrace
meant for prestigious good-trouble makers like Ilhan Omar and
    Ayanna Pressley.

Douse the pan with trustworthy oils, like macsaro (sesame),
    like olive.
Use a deep ladle to gather the right amount of dough.
Pour the dough for your first canjeero.
Choose the right size of canjeero to feed the root of your
    hunger today.

Let your canjeero spiral into the circle of life.
Let a thousand bubbles rise like prayers for each of your breaths.
Let it golden to life's sweetest ratio:
one part pain, one part generosity, and one part mother nature.

Layer your canjeero in a plate worthy of you.
Sprinkle bits of sugar, douse with a bit of sesame seed oil,
let the oil seep in the bubbly prayer crowns of your canjeero.

Let a steamy cup of shaah (tea) accompany your canjeero.

Now, your canjeero is ready.

Soon you will know why each canjeero
tastes differently deep within your soul.

You see:
Some canjeeroes are **firm** affirmation of generations
who never say *I love you*, yet who took bullets for you
and who carried you across oceans,
leaving the worlds they knew behind.

Some canjeeroes are **sweet** to give you fleeting joy breaks
    in the midst of unwavering racially pandemic times.

Some canjeeroes are **sour** truths of rising brown children in
    America who grew allergic to their own ethnic foods yet
    worship fast-food restaurant chains like gods.

Some canjeeroes are **thin** nicknames to never challenge the
    comfort sustaining whiteness.

Some canjeeroes are **thick** tales of fables and Dhegdheer
    and Arewalo
to keep your ethnic tongue twisting beyond the English language,
to keep you connected to your ancestors' wisdom.

Some canjeeroes are **crunchy** cures to replenish your black spirit.

Some canjeeroes are **sticky** light-skinning products to keep you
  from reaching your own self-healing blackness.

As COVID-19 actualizes our greatest fears
and magnifies our humanity's brokenness,
as the earth opens up to swallow millions
of grandparents around the world,

lean into the living wisdom coded in the food recipes of your
  ancestors.

My canjeero is a portal to my grandmother's oral love,
to her quiet petite spirit always bowing to the earthly land,
to her unwavering stubborn ways to stand up to injustices,

to the goodbye I never got to say,

to the timeless
touchless
rageful griefs
we will all carry
so heavily in our throats.

. . . .

Ifrah Mansour is a Somali, refugee, Muslim, multimedia artist and an educator based in Minnesota. Her artwork explores
trauma through the eyes of children to uncover the resiliencies
of blacks, Muslims, and refugees by interweaving poetry, pup-
petry, films, and installations. Her work includes the play *How to
Have Fun in a Civil War,* the exhibition *Can I Touch It,* the visual
poem *I Am a Refugee,* and the mixed-media installation *My Aqal,
Banned and Blessed.*

Living with the Dead

· · · · · · · · · · · · · · · · ·

May Lee-Yang

When I was a kid, every time we had an ua neeb or a spirit-calling ceremony, Dad fed his parents. He sat at the kitchen table with a bowl of rice, a bowl of boiled chicken, and an empty plate. As though my grandparents were here and not on the Other Side, he scooped a spoonful of rice, tore off a piece of chicken, and poured broth onto the plate. He repeated this, uttering words beneath his breath. I wondered: *How did he know how to do this? What were the words he uttered? Who would feed him when he was gone?*

One spring, Uncle Duck called me out of the blue.

"Your dad contacted Auntie and wants me to pass on a message," he said.

"What does he want?" I asked.

"He said he's been trying to contact all of your brothers and sisters, but no one is getting the message."

"Of course not," I told Uncle. None of us siblings were shamans, and we didn't know how to interpret dreams and visions either.

For the previous two weeks, I'd been feeling something amiss in my house. I'd walk past the kitchen and think someone was standing there. But when I looked more closely, the kitchen was empty. Or I'd be sitting in the living room and feel as if someone were nearby—again, usually in the kitchen, a room I could see from my usual spot on my armchair. Was Dad trying to make contact in these moments?

"Your dad said he's having trouble crossing over to the Other Side," said Uncle Duck. "He has too many debts to pay off. He wants your auntie to help him pass on."

Auntie Duck, whose real name I don't know, once told me she is like a telephone.

"When spirits need to communicate with our world, they borrow my voice to speak," she said. "Just like an interpreter."

Uncle Duck said Dad had been floating around the Other Side these past three years. Then Dad remembered Auntie Duck's abilities.

"You kids need to do an ua neeb so he can move on," he said.

"I understand," I told him. "I'll talk to the others and see what we can do."

As a child, if you asked me what was the difference between an ua neeb and a hu plig, I would have said, "When someone ua neeb"—since these are also verbs—"it's very boring. The only thing you get to eat is boiled pork with greens. There aren't that many people who come, and because of that there are no kids to play with and fewer cans of pop."

Hu plig ceremonies, however, were more fun. Usually a family kills a cow, so there are more things to eat. There would be laab, ground beef mixed with roasted rice powder, tripe, cilantro, green onions, peppers, and plenty of lime juice. You could eat it raw or cooked, and it was accompanied by platters of lettuce leaves and celery stalks. There was kua quav, a stew made of small pieces of beef, chopped-up intestines, liver, and ginger. It doesn't sound good, but it's delicious soul food. There might also be beef and ginger boiled until the meat was so soft it fell off the bones. If a pig had been sacrificed too, we could have a pork stir-fry of ginger and green onions. Perhaps there might be nqaij qab zib, chunks of pork stewed in a sweet syrup of oyster sauce, soy sauce, and sugar and finished off with whole boiled eggs.

Food was the only thing I enjoyed about hu plig and ua neeb ceremonies. Most of the time, they happened in houses too small to hold all the visiting relatives. There were usually no places to sit, and the homes were always loud with the sound of gongs, chanting, running children, and adults talking over each other. On any given weekend, there could be hundreds of ua neeb and hu plig ceremonies going on, and you are always expected to attend if possible.

"If you don't go help someone else," my mother said, "when you have an ua neeb or hu plig, who will come help you?"

As an adult now, I know some ua neeb and hu plig ceremonies are held to heal the sick, some to call back a lost spirit. Some are celebrations of weddings, births, and graduations, which end in tying white strings of yarn over the wrist of the person of honor. Some people went to these events to look good, to show how industrious and hardworking they are. Others went to socialize.

As a teenager, I went to very few ua neeb and hu plig ceremonies. Had I been cool enough, I might have been a goth teen, but since it was the nineties and I was poor, I was merely a homebody. My mother gave up trying to make me go to relatives' houses. After I got married, my husband and I rarely went. Mostly we didn't know when hu plig and ua neeb ceremonies happened, and eventually we only attended those by close family members.

Because my family moved from place to place, I have no childhood home to return to. When I was in sixth grade, my parents bought a house in Frogtown, but we later learned ghosts lingered there. When I was sixteen and woke up to baby ghost hands on my chest, we packed up and abandoned that house within the week. Over the years, my family roamed throughout St. Paul. My brother Pao's current house was a rental, but it was here that Dad lived his final years. It was here that we would do the ceremony to help him pay off his debts on the Other Side.

Because I was an outsider, a married daughter, a member of the Yang clan now instead of the Lee one, and because I am not a morning person, I arrived shortly after 9 AM with my husband, Peter. Though Pao was married, my sister Lisa, six years my junior, was more like the housewife, organizing food, people, and logistics. When we arrived, other people were already there and working: my brother Xin and his wife, my cousin Geno and his wife, my cousin Kong and his wife, and nieces and nephews who ranged from six months to thirty years of age.

In the living room, the couch and armchair were pushed against the walls. A temporary shaman's altar was created by placing an end table against one wall. On the end table were two mugs filled with uncooked jasmine rice, four shot glasses filled with water, a pile of unlit joss sticks, a cow horn split in two, and a set of finger ring bells. Above the end-table-turned-altar, a rectangular joss paper was taped on the wall. On the ground was a bucket of uncooked rice. Auntie Duck unpacked her shaman gear from an embroidered bag and stuck a carved wooden sword into the bucket of rice. She had another knife, this one made of steel, which she also placed sharp end down into the rice bucket. Last, she placed her rattle, a metallic circle with coins attached, between the swords.

Before the altar was a bench polished into a waxy veneer. Behind the bench was an area rug covered with black garbage bags taped onto the floor. At Auntie and Uncle Duck's directions, four guys carried in two pigs, freshly butchered that morning from the Long Cheng slaughterhouse, and laid them on the tarp. One was an adult-size pig, the second a smaller one. Somewhere there were six chickens: three male, three female, per Auntie Duck's order. These were all sacrifices.

Before she died, Grandma once told me why she never converted to Christianity. In Laos, missionaries visited their village.

"They told us to give money to their god," she said. "But you know what? If you're a Christian and donate money, you don't see where your money goes to. If you practice shamanism, every time you have a spirit-calling ceremony and butcher a cow or a pig, everyone gets to eat."

Grandma was a shaman.

I like to think that I'm special, that I have a place in my dad's heart because of two memories. The first involves ice cream trucks. As a child, I loved ice cream and the sound of ice cream trucks. To this day, when I smell exhaust fumes, I immediately think of cherry and banana Popsicles because twenty-five-cent Popsicles were the only things we bought from the trucks.

But there was a day when we were living in Stockton and the sun was about to set and an ice cream truck drove through our neighborhood for one last round of sales. Dad and I approached the truck, and I pointed hopefully to the Pac-Man ice-cream bar, which cost over a dollar.

Hmong people often said, "If you can't buy enough for everyone, don't buy anything at all."

For some reason, on this day, none of the other little kids were around, so Dad bought me the Pac-Man ice cream, and we both silently agreed not to let the other kids know.

My second memory is around this same time period. I had started preschool but did not want to go. Every morning I threw a fit, but Dad said, "Will you go if I buy you a hamburger?"

That got me every time. He drove to Hamburger Stand, Stockton's version of White Castle. The building was plain and white, but hamburgers were fifty-nine cents each and cheeseburgers sixty-nine cents, much more affordable than McDonald's or Burger King. Each morning I threw a fit, and each morning Dad took me to Hamburger Stand as a bribe.

"You're spoiled," said my mother, and I turned up my nose at her, not realizing this special treatment would not last forever.

· · · · · · · · ·

In the kitchen, women cooked, cleaned, or played games on their smartphones. In the backyard, little kids played in the patch of grass made muddy from that morning's storm. In another corner, guys stood before a circular barbecue grill, smoking, drinking green bottles of Rolling Rock beer, and occasionally burning joss paper boats so that Dad could pay his debts on the Other Side. This was spirit money, after all.

On the back deck, Lisa set up a canopy to cover worktables and coolers of bottled water, pop, and beer. Two propane tanks sat in the corner of the deck attached to an outdoor single-burner stove top. A giant wok rested on the stove top waiting to be used.

Peter and I had no real duties. Technically, as members of the Yang clan, we were outsiders. That aside, Peter didn't know how to chop meat properly, and I didn't like touching the offal. Instead, we took a four-year-old nephew to Target to buy Hatchimal toys and treats. We returned to my brother's house with Starbucks coffee and three selections of ice cream: Drumsticks, sandwiches, and Push-Up Pops. I passed the time watching YouTube solar system songs with a two-year-old nephew while Peter held a nine-month-old one. We occasionally mediated fights among the ten-year-olds.

Then Auntie Duck asked all the Lee family members to congregate by the bench in front of the altar.

"Sorry," my cousin Geno said. "You and Peter don't count."

"I'm fine," I said. I don't get offended by Hmong protocols like this. If I cared about Hmong protocols, I would have helped to cook and clean, or pretended to, anyway.

Every immediate family member who was still a Lee squeezed on, by, or around the bench in the living room. A few people clutched shirts belonging to other family members who weren't present so those members could be blessed or whatever it was Auntie Duck was doing. Auntie corralled everyone with a string, walked around them, and uttered words I couldn't understand.

Then she sipped water from a bowl and spat it at people from three different angles.

Years ago when Peter and I went to my father-in-law's house for a spirit-calling ceremony, we ran into one of his relatives. This relative was a pastor, but out of respect he attended shamanistic family events. On the walk to my father-in-law's house, the reverend said, "Have you two thought about converting? Church is much easier for the younger generation than these Hmong ceremonies."

Church meant you didn't have to wake up early on weekends to go help cook and clean at some relative's house.

Church meant you could dress nicely instead of wearing aprons over clothes that could afford to be splashed by animal blood or egg roll grease.

But church also meant early mornings *every* Sunday. Church meant genuinely believing in God, because I had no intentions of being a half-assed Christian.

"Thanks for asking," said Peter, "but we're good."

In the last year of his life, I visited Dad not as often I wished. I wanted to take him to Hawaii in a last-ditch effort to show him the world. I settled for renting a three-level vacation home in Wisconsin Dells and invited family members to come hang out. Over the weekend, forty of us representing three generations of one family ate, drank, and swam in a private cabana with our own hot tub. My oldest brother, Tou, took Dad to the movies, something I'd never seen the two of them do together before. I looked like a baller when, in truth, I footed the bill through funds from a fellowship.

In the last year of Dad's life, I went over to my brother Pao's house and painted with Dad, ate with him, and had generic conversations with him. Once in a while, we got somewhere deep.

I once asked Dad about his two names. Legally, his name was

Wang Phia and his OG name—in theory, a more dignified name
to show one's rank as a husband, father, and leader—was Nom
Yeej, "one who will win or conquer." I always found it odd that
Wang Phia, which I assumed was his birth name, was so formal.

"No, my original name was Toua," said Dad.

Toua? This was like finding out Benedict Timothy Carlton
Cumberbatch's real name was Ben Cumber. Toua seemed like
such a humble name for a man with as much ambition and pre-
tension as my dad. But I suppose it matched him. He was an
orphan who started with nothing and eventually had soldiers
under his command. He later became a provincial leader.

"Why'd you change your name?" I asked.

"Because my first wife had become a zombie and was coming
after me."

He didn't exactly say "zombie," but he *did* say "poj ntxhoog." A
poj ntxhoog was not like a spirit, a being one cannot touch. A poj
ntxhoog was flesh and blood, dead but still moving about.

When Dad's first wife died, they laid her out on a low bamboo
cot in preparation for her burial. But at night, he heard someone
walking around the perimeter of his hut, scratching the walls.

"I never saw her," he said. "But I knew she was out there."

They changed his name to Wang Phia Lee so that First Wife
wouldn't be able to find him.

I knew Dad was dying. He had been in the process of dying since
I was sixteen.

That year I got a phone call that Dad had driven his car into a
pole and ended up in the ICU. He was on life support. After I got
off the phone, I went straight to my typewriter and began record-
ing a dream I'd had two nights before.

In the dream, Dad and I were working in a factory with metal
conveyer belts curving everywhere. All of a sudden, he collapsed
and died. Then the dream rewound itself. Before Dad entered the
factory, I walked over to a woman standing a few feet away.

"In a few minutes, my dad will fall over," I told her. "Please help him, so he doesn't die."

I woke up before I could see if she helped him or not.

At the hospital, I learned my brothers had similar dreams. Houa dreamt that he and Dad were on top of a cliff. Dad fell down, and Houa drove his car circling the cliffside, trying to reach Dad before he hit the bottom. Houa woke up before he saw the end. My brother Xin dreamt that someone chased Dad around with a knife trying to kill him. He too didn't know the outcome of the dream.

Dad eventually recovered from the car accident, but he got his license revoked. While all of us went to work, went to school, or even played, he was stuck at home. Eventually, he started to speak to people who weren't there. Pictures of Hmong politicians who had abandoned him. Signs from white Republicans who never knew him. The TV static. Us children too.

One day when I was in my thirties, Peter and I went to take Dad out to lunch. He came out of the house not because of us but because a fifteen-passenger van had come to pick him up.

"What's going on?" I asked.

"Today Dad usually goes to a Hmong adult day center," said Lisa. I remembered stories about this. Dad occasionally went to hang out with other Hmong elders. Sometimes he came home with toilet paper or bags of rice—prizes he earned from playing bingo and other games.

Dad's gaze shifted between me and the van.

"Go with the old people," I told him. "We can go out to lunch another day."

I'd spent all of my adult life avoiding old people who were always asking things like: *Who are you? Who are your parents? How come I've never heard of you before? Do you have kids? If you don't have kids, your husband will abandon you. Do you do housework? If you don't do housework, your husband will abandon you.*

Instead, I spent my work life delivering programs to teens around sexual health, leadership development, and the arts.

But suddenly I was inspired. Wouldn't it be cool to start a theater program for Hmong elders to gather their stories, to create a platform for them to share their stories with younger people in a more engaging way?

Inspired by Dad, I dreamed up a program called Letters to Our Grandchildren. This was in March. In November, I was funded for the program. In December, Dad died. In February, on the day after we buried Dad, I started the program without him.

I was sitting in the kitchen trying to coax my two-year-old nephew to go to sleep when Uncle Duck said, "You guys wanna hear some last words from your dad? You gotta come now."

Peter and I went into the living room. My brothers Pao and Xin were already sitting on the couch listening. Lisa joined us and closed the sliding door that separated the living room from the kitchen.

Auntie Duck sat on the bench, facing the altar, her head covered in a black scarf. Each of her hands held the finger bells, which resembled metallic cake donuts. They rang as her thighs moved up and down. She chanted in rhythm. She chanted in rhyme. Some words I understood. Some I didn't. Sometimes the words became a song. Sometimes she can be possessed. Sometimes a spirit is so angry it takes over her body instead of letting her interpret.

I couldn't tell if Auntie Duck was possessed by Dad or just relaying his words. As in life, his words got muddled. My Hmong wasn't good enough to catch all the nuances and metaphors. Even when Dad was alive and I was sitting across the table from him asking questions, we could not speak.

But there was a time when we understood each other. When

I was eight and woke up in the middle of the night hungry (but really, I was just bored), he made me a midnight meal of rice and water and gingerroot dipped in salt. Sometimes there was just salt.

"When we lived in Laos, we were so poor that this was sometimes all we ate," he said. I was too young then to feel pity, shame, or sadness about the scarcity of food in Laos. I was also too young to know that salt was a luxury.

Back then, I'm not sure how we spoke, but we understood each other clearly.

By the time I was thirteen, I was ashamed he could not speak English and was angry he almost let my counselors put me in ESL class because he didn't know better. Before my racist counselor could sign me up for remedial courses, I intervened and was promptly put in higher-level classes. When I was seventeen, I cursed Dad, angry that he sent hundreds of dollars every month to pay for a fifteen-year mortgage for a house that didn't exist in Laos.

"You're getting conned by your stupid Hmong leaders," I told him.

"I'm trying to get back our homeland, so we can return one day," he said.

"You're never going back!"

And he couldn't. As a soldier in the Secret War, there was a price on his head. He could never return to Laos, even as a tourist.

When I was in my twenties and tried to collect his story, I asked questions in broken Hmonglish.

Thaum koj nyob pem Nplog teb, what did you do?

Koj muaj tshawg tus brothers *thiab* sisters?

Did you *pais kawm ntawv*?

And though he wanted to respond, he couldn't always do it.

Sometimes we couldn't find the right vocabulary between Hmong and English.

Sometimes he didn't know the answer. How do you tell someone your opinion when no one has asked for your opinion in thirty years?

And sometimes his memory was not clear.

Once he told me he loved playing the qeej, a reed pipe.

"I would have been a great qeej player, but Grandpa smoked opium, you see. When he asked me if he could sell my qeej for opium, I said yes."

"Were you angry at your father?" I asked.

One time he told me he was angry at Grandpa. I would be angry at Grandpa too for being a drug addict, for taking Dad's qeej, for dying early and leaving Dad an orphan, for dying early so Grandma married someone else, leaving Dad further abandoned.

But another time he said, "No. I loved my father, so of course I let him sell my qeej."

I still don't know which was the correct version of the story.

In the month between a person's death and their funeral, we hold daily wakes where friends and family come to visit. This is to keep the house "warm," but the reality is that the family is too busy to grieve. They spend the wake slaughtering animals, cooking, cleaning, and entertaining the visitors. It was on such a day during my mother's wake that Pao and I sat in the basement of their house. We were on opposite sides of a rectangular table surrounded by a sea of empty folding chairs.

I said to Pao, "I'm sorry you had to give up your dreams to take care of Dad."

I didn't even know what Pao's dreams were. When we were teenagers, Dad started suffering from schizophrenia and PTSD. I went off to college, got married, and chased my dreams. Pao and the younger siblings stayed home, worked, and watched over Dad. Then when Mother got sick unexpectedly, they watched her die.

"If you want to take some time to chase your dreams, go back to school or something, let me know," I said. "I'll help make it happen."

"I don't want you to feel sorry for me," he said. "I don't ever regret taking care of Dad. I'm glad I'm here for him."

And I felt ashamed because, had we traded places, I knew I would have lived with regret.

What kind of human being was I that I lived with so much shame and regret?

Growing up, I never hated the taste of Hmong food, but I was embarrassed to eat it in public. A niece who is at least fifteen years younger than me once declared, "I've never been ashamed of my food," but we lived in different times. When I was young, eating American fast food was a luxury. When I was young, there were few if any Hmong restaurants in town. When I was young, non-Hmong people made fun of us, assuming people like me spoke no English or ate dogs. I strived to be as American as possible, to give white people no excuse to call me out. I wanted to blend in, and that meant no Hmong food in public.

My first year of college, I lived an hour away from home, and dorm life meant American food all the time: bagels and cream cheese for breakfast, grilled cheese sandwiches and Jell-O for lunch, the occasional bad Asian stir-fry for dinner. Most of the time, I skipped out on the cafeteria and made my own dinner in the basement kitchen of my dorm. On occasion, my Hmong friends and I walked to the local grocery store and bought whole rotisserie chickens, which we ate with rice and grieved that there was no chili pepper sauce accompaniment. Then one weekend I went home, and before I returned to my dorm, my mother handed me a paper bag.

"Take these back with you," she said.

I looked inside and saw plastic bags filled with egg rolls, laab, salad with a Hmong egg yolk dressing, vermicelli noodles with ground pork and herbs, stewed pork and boiled eggs, rice, and chili pepper sauce. These were leftovers from a hu plig she had attended earlier that day.

"I can't eat all of this," I told her.

"Bring it with you anyway," she told me.

When the other Hmong students on campus heard I had hu plig leftovers, they all ran to my dorm room. I watched as they devoured everything, and even though I had told my mother I would probably not eat anything, I joined in on the meal, suddenly protective of the food.

"You hit the jackpot," said one friend. They'd all been hungry for Hmong food, and suddenly I realized what I had taken for granted.

By 2:30 PM Auntie Duck was done with the ceremony. I wondered if the ceremony worked. Would Dad be able to cross over? Would he finally be at peace? Or would I continue to feel a presence in my kitchen and wonder if it was him?

In the kitchen and backyard, people scrambled to finish turning the pigs into boiled pork with mustard greens, deep-fried pork, and pork and bamboo stir-fry. More nieces and nephews showed up to wash dishes and watch kids. People passed around cans of beer, but no one got shit-faced drunk. Everyone was trying to be respectful to my dad. In the backyard, the guy cousins and nephews continued burning joss paper boats to Dad.

As I looked around, it occurred to me that, at forty-one, my cousin Kong was the oldest person here. My husband, Peter, at thirty-eight, was the second-oldest person in the house. Trailing Peter by one month was me. All of the elders were gone: Mom and Dad had been dead for years. Grandma had passed on just two months before. One older sibling was vacationing in Vietnam. Two others were attending a wedding in Walnut Grove.

"There are no old people here," I told Peter.

"*We're* the old people," he corrected.

And it was true. We were all still alive and still taking care of our dead.

. . . .

May Lee-Yang is a Minnesota-based Hmong American writer, performance artist, and teacher. Her theater works include *The Korean Drama Addict's Guide to Losing Your Virginity*, *Confessions of a Lazy Hmong Woman*, and *Ten Reasons Why I'd Be a Bad Porn Star*. Her artmaking has been supported by the Playwrights' Center McKnight Fellowship, the Jerome Foundation, the National Performance Network, the Bush Foundation, the Minnesota State Arts Board, and the Loft Literary Center. She has an MFA in creative writing from the University of Minnesota.

Haitian Kitchen

. . . .

Valérie Déus

At the bodega down the block from my house, the owner eyes me picking up the plantains.

"Where are you from?" asks the store clerk suspiciously while I pick out three green plantains.

"My parents are from Haiti," I say, and his suspicion turns into a smile.

"Oh! Haiti?! So, you know what to do with those," he responds confidently.

I nod and say, "Yes, this is my food."

Haitians are serious about food. It's not a surprise, considering many of our parents have stories about food insecurity as part of their upbringing. I grew up in the United States, but once I crossed the threshold of my family home, I was in my parents' version of Haiti.

When I lived in New York City, I always had access to Caribbean staples to make Haitian food. If I didn't want to eat my mother's cooking, there were countless restaurants I could call on for a quick Haitian fix. If I wanted Haitian patties, a croissant-like flakey baked good filled with minced meat or shredded salted codfish, I could go to Le Bon Pain in Queens. If I wanted a Haitian meal, there was Grandchamps in Brooklyn or countless other places. Although I've met quite a few Haitians here in Minnesota, Haitian food is still elusive—I miss biskuit sec, pain jabon, AK100, kasav, tablet, and legim ak krab, and special occasion patties. I call them special occasion patties because that's when they taste the best; they are made for a first communion, a party, a repas after a funeral—those patties are super delicious.

I moved to Minneapolis several years ago and brought with me all of the Haitian cooking traditions my mother tried her best to instill in me. I needed plantains, sour oranges, keneps, and all the delicious foods I grew up with; the foods I could find weren't the same quality that I was used to at home. Mangoes never smelled mango-like—they were rarely sweet and mainly on the tart side. Plantains were spotty, thin, and dull. And I could never get ten limes for a dollar like I could at any supermarket in NYC. For a while, I had my uncle send me mangoes and sugarcane from his garden in Florida, and my mother sent me care packages of things I couldn't get.

Moving here wasn't easy culturally, especially when it came to food, and early on I could barely find a plantain at my local supermarket. Being away from home became a test to see if I had really absorbed those cooking lessons, and I learned quickly that some lessons stuck, but some didn't.

I found my first plantains at ALDI on Lake Street, and it was like finding buried treasure. I was excited and proud to share my food with my new cohabitants. It had been so long since I last had them that I opted for the short method of preparation: no double-frying with a salt water bath in between. They were a delicious golden piece of home and settled my stomach after a long stretch of American fare.

When I'm cooking Haitian food, I am in communion with my mother, my grandma, and all of my foremothers. I hear my mother's voice guiding me as I hold a thick plantain in my hand, find the vein, and run the knife down the side without splitting the flesh. I cut it into diagonal slices and fry them up. If I'm not in the frying mood, I leave the skin on, cut the whole plantain across the middle so I have two pieces, and make a slit in the skin to accommodate expansion when I boil it. It's like being in church, taking part in a spiritual act that grounds me in the entirety of who I am. It brings me back to family meals and special family dinners from my childhood. Food is history, memory, and love. It brings me back to all the celebrations and good times we've had.

What settles my stomach and comforts my mouth are my cultural foods. I can fool my belly for only so long before I need my food.

Cooking my traditional foods in the way my mother taught me is about ritual. It's the only religion that speaks to my spirit. Of course, that doesn't mean I don't use modern methods to puree my spices or I don't use limes if I can't find sour oranges or lemons. Fried plantains are a quick and easy introduction to my cultural foods. Some people like to fry up the yellow-almost-brown plantains. I don't go for them unless I'm putting them on ice cream (totally try it!). If I'm frying plantains I'm going to eat with my meal, then I go for the yellow-but-still-firm plantains. They hold up well during the frying, and they are a great combination of sweet and starchy. You can also fry green plantains; they are yummy too.

Fried Plantains / Banan Peze

I've been frying plantains since I was little. It's usually the first thing you learn how to cook, and it's usually served with griot.

2 plantains, green or slightly yellow but still firm
2 cups oil
½ cup water
1 teaspoon salt
2 plates, one big and one small

Cut off the ends of plantains and slide your knife down the body of the plantain along a vein. Cut plantain into 1½-inch-thick diagonal pieces.

Heat oil in a skillet over medium heat. Cook plantains in hot oil for about 3 minutes on each side or until they are light brown. Keep the pan hot.

Remove plantains from heat and place them on the big plate. Using the bottom of the small plate, gently flatten the plantains and set them aside.

In a small bowl mix the water and the salt and dip each plantain in the mixture.

Cook the plantains in the skillet until golden brown and crispy on both sides.

Remove plantains from the pan and place on some paper towels to remove excess oil.

I continued my search for Haitian food in Minnesota and found salted dried cod at a Southeast Asian market in the suburbs. Cod was introduced to Haiti via Portuguese slave traders (hence my family's last name), and salted codfish and boiled plantains was one of my favorite meals growing up. My mother made mori ak banan on the weekends for a quick meal. She always soaked the codfish overnight, changing the water frequently before boiling it to start the cooking process.

Salted Codfish / Mori

½ pound salted codfish
1–2 tablespoons oil
½ onion, chopped
½ bell pepper, chopped
1 shallot, minced
1–2 cloves garlic, minced
¼ teaspoon tomato paste

Soak fish in water for at least 2 hours, changing the water at least twice.

Boil fish to further desalt. Taste to make sure it's not too salty.

Drain and shred fish, removing any small bones.

Heat oil in a skillet; add fish, onions, bell peppers, shallot, and garlic and cook, stirring, over low heat.

Stir in tomato paste, then add ½ cup water. Let simmer for 20 minutes.

I left my home in a New York that was filled with reflections of my Haitian culture at every turn and moved to Minnesota to be with my husband and his family.

Moving to a part of the country where my primary culture isn't represented was harder than I initially expected. In so many ways, being a hyphenated American is about straddling both worlds. You live in the hyphen. You don't realize how much of one or the other you are until you're in a context outside of your regular world.

Sometimes my mother-in-law would ask about my food traditions. Initially I was open and eager to talk about my culture and its relationship to food, and I would share online recipes, figuring this was a way for us to connect.

My first attempt to share was plantains, since they are easy and delicious. I fried both green and yellow to show the difference in taste and texture. While the family seemed to enjoy them, my husband's mother kept calling them *plantations*, instead of plantains.

Food usually helps people from different cultures connect, but somehow my mother-in-law found a way to "other" me through food. I've never asked her why she would do that because I learned early that confronting a Minnesotan is a fool's errand. The deflecting, defending, denial, and gaslighting isn't worth it. Maintaining my food tradition and not drowning in a sea of hamburgers and hot dogs has become a type of resistance for me. Food is resistance, and I just refuse to let the things I love about myself disappear for the sake of blending in. Roses aren't mad that tulips aren't like them, violets aren't mad that peonies are different from them, yet some people feel this impulse to harass "the different" people into being like them, a cultlike need to force folks into the fold.

So instead, I chose to ignore her insult and vowed never to share my food with her again. Haitian food is all over the internet.

If she's really interested, she can do the work and find the info there. I'm no one's Google.

My response to these attempts at micro-colonization is to not cook for the family when requested to. For occasions when we're asked to contribute, my husband will usually prepare something to share with family.

One of my mother's lessons that comes through regardless of what I'm making is cleaning my meat. My differences with my MIL were illustrated when it came to cooking meat. I clean meat with a sour citrus, whether it be lemon, lime, or sour oranges, also known as zorang su. I favor lemon or lime since zorang su aren't easy to find in Minnesota. When I was a kid in Brooklyn, we could buy zorang su at any Korean grocer.

My MIL loves to quote the FDA about the cultural practice of cleaning meats with citrus. When she does, I wonder what the FDA has to say about lutefisk—but I'm sure she doesn't know. It never fails, any time I had to cook for a family event, she would inevitably find a way to scrutinize and dismiss my cooking methods.

After twelve years of marriage, I've figured out my boundaries regarding my food and my in-laws, and I figure since they didn't marry me, they don't get to eat my food. Sharing myself and who I am isn't mandatory, so I don't. I won't say there's no tension around my decision and boundaries, but it helps me survive the passive-aggressive planet called Minnesota.

Cleaning meat and seasoning food are part of my cultural makeup. My methods aren't better than anyone else's; they're just a part of who I am and how I was raised. I sometimes wonder why my traditions are such a challenge for my MIL. Why does the way I clean and give thanks to chicken bother her? It's interesting and somewhat amusing. The idea that there is only one proper way to do something doesn't leave room for appreciating other people's ideas and innovations. It's limiting.

Cultural traditions aren't about claiming superiority. They're just different ideas from different people. The American binary way of thinking invades every aspect of life—things are either black or white, good or bad. But growing up within a predominantly Caribbean culture, I know that the truth of living is in the gray, in the mixture. We accept that life is gray and move on. We don't beat ourselves up about it, hide it, or lie to ourselves about it.

Haitian Meat Cleaning Process: Chicken

Remove the skin and all the excess and visible fat.

Scrub the meat with sliced limes or sour oranges, and place the meat and fruit slices in a bowl.

Pour boiling water into the bowl, making sure the water covers every piece of meat, and let sit for 30–45 seconds.

Drain and rinse with cool water while removing any leftover fat.

Add lime juice and seasoning to the meat.

When I first started living with my husband, he was fascinated with the way I stocked the kitchen: limes, lemons, bouillon cubes, bay leaves, a variety of spices, including several types of salt and pepper, a giant sack of rice, etc. I think he dreamed I would be cooking elaborate Haitian meals every night, but he's come to realize I only cook Haitian when my heart is in it. Otherwise, it's tacos. LOL.

My husband says he loves many things about me, and I'm sure my Haitian cooking is one of them. He hates leftovers and will refuse to eat something he loved the day before—unless it's Haitian food. The combination of spices brings out flavors he clearly wasn't used to, and I believe the food is more delicious the next day once the flavors get a chance to really sink into the meal. My husband always ate my mother's cooking with great enthusiasm, and she loved to watch him eat. I also make sure not to cook Haitian food too often, since I know only a limited number of recipes. When I cook Haitian food, it's *special*.

From the scotch bonnet pepper bite of pikliz to the flaky layers of a pâté, I can tell you my life's story through Haitian food.

My husband will say that I don't cook often (sorry not sorry, Mom) but when I do, it's usually for self-care, to commemorate someone or something, or to celebrate an achievement. American food is for regular life. In my house, it's just everyday living. Haitian food is special-occasion food, celebrating-the-self food, memory food, my spiritual food. If I am willing to spend the time it takes to make a Haitian meal for you, then you must be important to me.

January 1 is the day Haitians celebrate their independence from French colonial rule, and part of that celebration is making and enjoying soup joumou, Haitian pumpkin soup. The soup was originally enjoyed only by the French colonizers because it was forbidden for the enslaved Haitians. So on January 1, 1804, Haitians celebrated their liberty by drinking a bowl of this forbidden soup.

Once the Haitians won their independence, Jean-Jacques Dessalines commemorated the victory by having a bowl of this prohibited soup as a celebratory act of rebellion. The soup immediately became a symbol of freedom, and now almost every Haitian family has soup joumou on Independence Day. That was the version of the story my parents told me, but there are other versions. The soup's history wasn't written down, but the spirit of the soup remains.

Soup Joumou

1 cup distilled white vinegar
2 cups lime juice (keep rinds)
1 pound beef shank, meat cut off bones in ½-inch pieces
1 pound beef chuck, cut in ½-inch pieces
1 cup epis (Google a recipe for Haitian epis)
1 tablespoon seasoned salt
oil for frying
1 pound beef bones

2 pounds calabaza, giraumon, or butternut squash, cut into big chunks
10 cups low-sodium beef stock
3 medium potatoes, cubed
3 cups shredded cabbage
2 carrots, peeled and sliced
1 celery stalk, cut in ½-inch pieces
2 medium turnips, cubed
1 large onion, diced
5 whole cloves
3 sprigs parsley
¼ teaspoon thyme
¼ teaspoon salt
½ teaspoon black pepper
½ cup dried spaghetti
½ cup dried rigatoni
1 tablespoon Beurre Lily Chaloner or oil

In a medium bowl, pour vinegar and 1 cup of lime juice on beef shank and chuck beef. Rub meat with rinds. Rinse meat with lukewarm water and set aside.

In a new bowl, add epis seasoning, remaining lime juice, seasoned salt, and beef and mix together. Let marinate overnight.

In a large pot, heat oil until sizzling. Add meat and bones and brown on all sides; set aside.

Place pumpkin or squash in a pot with water to cover. Bring to a boil and cook until fork-tender, 20–25 minutes; drain. Using tongs or a slotted spoon, scoop out the flesh and transfer squash to a blender. Add 4 cups of broth and puree until smooth. Return to the pot and bring to a simmer.

Add 4 cups of broth and browned beef and bones; cover and simmer for about 40 minutes.

Add potatoes, cabbage, carrots, celery, turnips, onions, cloves, parsley, thyme, salt, pepper, and remaining 2 cups of broth. Simmer, uncovered, until vegetables are tender, 30–35 minutes.

Add the pasta and Buerre Lily or oil. Cover pot, lower heat to a simmer, and cook for 20 minutes. Stir occasionally; taste and adjust the seasoning.

· · · · · · · · ·

Because of the patriarchy, when dad cooks, it's seen as special or a treat. On TV, dads aren't supposed to know their way around a kitchen, yet somehow they expect to eat. My father knew how to cook. He cooked for himself in the years before he met my mom and continued to cook during the times early in my childhood when he picked me up from school. The afternoons we spent together eating and watching *Tom and Jerry* are some of my favorite childhood memories. During that time, on Sunday mornings my dad would make me and my mom codfish fritters, also known as accra de moru. My dad always called it marinade. My father whipped up these delicious fritters quickly, and they disappeared as fast. As I got older and my parents started to work more, the fritters stopped, but every couple of years I turned to him and asked, "Papi, do you remember when you used to make codfish fritters?" He would smile and say, "Oh, yes, that's a long, long time ago. Too much grease for me now."

Accra de Moru

½ cup soaked and finely shredded salted codfish (see below)
2 bay leaves, optional
1½ cups flour
1 cup water, plus more if necessary
½ tablespoon minced chives
½ tablespoon thinly chopped fresh parsley
1 clove garlic, minced
½ teaspoon ground thyme
1 egg, separated
½ teaspoon white vinegar
salt and pepper to taste
oil for frying
1–2 dashes baking soda

To prepare the codfish: Desalt the codfish for at least 12 hours in cold water, changing the water twice. Place codfish in a saucepan with water to cover; add bay leaves (if using), and bring to a boil. Simmer at least 30 minutes. Remove from water and let codfish cool before shredding and removing any bones.

In a large bowl, whisk together flour and water to make a very moist dough. Stir in shredded codfish and chives, parsley, garlic, and thyme. (If you want a homogeneous batter, pour mixture into a blender and blend for less than 1 minute.) Mix together beaten egg yolk and vinegar; stir into batter. Season with salt and pepper. Refrigerate mixture for at least 10 to 15 minutes.

Heat enough oil for batter. Remove batter from refrigerator; add baking soda and mix. Beat egg white to almost stiff. Add to batter and gently blend well.

Drop batter by spoonfuls into hot oil. Do not overload the pan. Cook until golden brown and crispy, turning once on each side. Drain fritters on a paper towel. Serve immediately.

Growing up, learning how to cook from my mother, I wasn't always the best or most attentive student. Many times, I was quite resistant to the idea of having to cook. It felt like servitude, and I figured since most chefs are men, I could just get me one of those. Eventually, I grew out of my eight-year-old thinking and ultimately learned more than my mother expected. Now, I'm not a Haitian cooking maven—I like to keep it simple in the kitchen—but I can handle the basics. Ultimately, I won't starve as long as I have rice, beans, epis, and plantains.

. . . .

Valérie Déus is a poet, radio show host, and film programmer. Her work has been featured in *Minnesota Women's Press, The Brooklyn Rail, Midway, Saint Paul Almanac, The BeZine,* and most recently in *A Garden of Black Joy: Global Poetry from the Edges of Liberation and Living* and *Under Purple Skies: The Minneapolis Anthology.* When she's not writing, she is the host of *Project 35,* a local low-fi radio show on KRSM featuring music from all over the diaspora plus poetry and conversation. She curates Film-North's Cinema Lounge and is the shorts programmer for the Provincetown International Film Festival.

An Unfortunate Mosaic

· · · · · · · · · · · · · · · ·

Michael Torres

There's a taco truck parked up the street from where I live. It's been there every day for the last few days. I can't say why its presence interests and even slightly bothers me. I think, because I want to lump it together with the other Mexican restaurants in a small town with an 89.9 percent white population, the taco truck, by default, makes a bad first impression.

The truck is plain white and on its side sports images of floating American food—hamburgers, french fries, hot dogs. It wasn't until I passed it on a run that I saw a menu for tacos and quesadillas.

Since moving to Minnesota from California in 2013, I've doubted any local Mexican restaurant that claims to be authentic. Maybe it is authentic. Maybe it's that each establishment puts that word in each ad, on the logo painted on the wall where you walk in.

During my third year living in Minnesota—as an aspiring writer, as an adjunct professor, and as a Mexican American—I received grant funding for a research trip to Mexico. In my application I wrote about wanting to see where my father grew up. I'd never been to Mexico except for the California border towns of my late teens and early twenties. But those don't count. I don't think they do, anyway. The way I understood it, towns like Rosarito and Tijuana catered to Americans looking for a bunch of fun and

41

the possibility of danger without it actually happening, all at a cheap price.

The trip I planned would include stays in Guadalajara and Mexico City, and would culminate with a two-week visit with my tio Ismael, my father's brother, whom I met when I was too young to remember. My tio had lived and worked in the United States—had legal papers, he would end up telling me—but returned to the pueblo of Yahualica to care for his elderly parents in the late nineties. I imagined my tio's family there to greet me. I thought: *I'm going home for the first time.* That spring before the trip, to prepare myself, I enrolled in a Spanish conversation class; I downloaded Duolingo; I listened to my Los Tigres del Norte Pandora station at least three times a week.

Maybe it's that every one of these Mexican restaurants in Mankato claims to be authentically Mexican and I, as a Mexican American, want to know how; I want proof.

The next week, the taco truck is still there, and planted in the dirt next to the parking lot are red- and green-lettered signs that spell TACO TRUCK. The lack of a name, the absence of any effort to imagine an identity for this food truck upsets me. At the red light, I notice a line snaked from the ordering window. It's busier than last time. But it doesn't have a name, so I'm not as easily fooled as those waiting for food. When the light turns green, I ease off the brake and watch the letters nod goodbye.

It's early July when I get to Mexico. I want to try their street tacos. Their beer. I want pan dulce in the mornings from the panaderia down the street from my hotel so that I can say to myself, *This reminds me of childhood.* I want dinner in the rich parts of the cities I visit for the day. I want what they have. I want the best churros in town.

· · · · · · · · · ·

From "Adventures in the Picturesque: Voyage and Voyeurism in the Tourist Guidebook to Mexico" by Persephone Braham: "The practice of tourism was born in the eighteenth century, a product of the vogue for the picturesque that was the inspiration for the peripatetic Romantics . . . the impulse toward the picturesque exemplified the modern obsession with objectification: it subjected nature to an ordering achieved through rationalized visual practices" (380).

On one of the first few days in Guadalajara, I find a crowd gathered in an open plaza between a row of shops. Men dressed as clowns perform tricks, flips, and magic. I get close. After a few minutes, two or three clowns walk the crowd. They remove their hats and, in a mock holdup, pull out bright plastic guns to point first at folks in the crowd, then to the bottom of the hat, so the tourists know where the tips go. I laugh and walk away with my hands behind my back.

The first thing I learned about Minnesota before moving here was how popular the state fair is. Both charming and odd are the butter sculptures—bust carvings made to resemble the latest Princess Kay of the Milky Way, whose role for the year, upon crowning, is to promote Minnesota's dairy industry.

In Mexico, I want routine. No matter the day's plan, I start with a morning run as if I live here.

One day, I meet a café owner who loves poetry, who is himself a poet. He loves Bukowski and Burroughs. On his wall a bumper sticker: *Por favor, lea poesía.* I ask, but he doesn't have any for sale. Before I leave, I buy his book, ask him to sign it. I buy a bar of soap his daughter sells out of a small box next to the cash register. Later, I'll follow his café's page on social media.

· · · · · · · · ·

"What used to be described in tourism as the desire for the picturesque, now is understood as a search for the 'authentic'—the found as opposed to the produced ... motivated by a desire for contact with the dangerous Other, whether it is embodied in nature or in culture.... Ironically, the search for authenticity is an inherently self-defeating one: the tourist follows the topography—both physical and cultural—represented in his guidebook, ultimately tracing, in the most prosaic and complete sense, his own image contained therein" (Braham, "Adventures in the Picturesque," 382).

It's been a few weeks since the arrival of Taco Truck. The letter signs still wave. It's late spring. Warmer, finally. I see customers fill the parking lot, order, and wait for their food. Now there's a banner covering the side of the truck, and I imagine the hot dogs and burgers underneath, getting soggy in the warm dark. The banner is essentially an ad for beer. Below the Pacifico emblem it reads: *Birria Tacos.* Below that: *Best tacos in town ... possibly the universe.*

I take a photo of a street vendor on a Sunday afternoon in Mexico City. In it, the elderly woman selling corn in a cup is only partially visible on the upper right corner of the frame. It's really just her face from the nose down. She's wearing a green blouse, sleeves rolled up. She seems grandmotherly to me, and perhaps that's why I think it would be easy to get a good photo. I try to get a shot of the roasted corn as she shaves cobs into a pan to be mixed with lemon and spices. I stand to her left, but close enough that when I lift the camera and snap the shot, she notices and gets mad at me for taking the photo. She yells something in Spanish. I back away nervous and also upset, which surprises me. I step back and look around to see if anyone's watching, if anyone sees me there too.

. . . .

"Just as the voyeuristic encounter is founded on dominance sustained by distance, the tourist's contact with the other has consequences that diminish foreignness and destroy authenticity" (Braham, "Adventures in the Picturesque," 391).

Taco Truck actually sits in the Charley's Restaurant & Lounge parking lot. During the pandemic of 2020, because Charley's menu, as noted in the *Mankato Free Press*, "is not conducive for take-out orders," the family-owned restaurant invested in a partnership with Alberto Lara, who worked under his family at El Mazatlan Mexican Restaurant. Lara, the article says, has dreamt of owning his own Mexican restaurant in Mankato since he moved from Los Angeles. When I read that last part about LA, I think, *we grew up half an hour from each other*, and then, *maybe I've seen him once, the few times I'd been to El Mazatlan.*

My tio Ismael arranges for his friend, a cab driver in Yahualica, to pick me up from the hotel in Guadalajara and drive me more than two hours back to my tio. Since I'd been listening to and attempting to speak Spanish for almost two weeks, I'm able to hold what could be considered a conversation, though it cracks in many places.

If you visit El Mazatlan's website you can watch their "story" through a two-minute YouTube video. It opens with traditional ranchera-style trumpet playing before the narrator, Karina Felix, tells us the restaurant opened in 2003 and is family-owned. A few moments later, a camera pans out over a busy restaurant at midday. Then it moves to a single family at a table, and one of the patrons summarizes his family's experience at El Mazatlan by saying, "It makes us feel like we're going on a miniature vacation." Then there's a montage of patron testimonies. They love the free chips and salsa. They love the enchiladas. The fajita burrito. Margaritas. Everyone loves that everything is authentic. At the end, Felix invites us to visit before the man who appreciates the miniature vacation returns for the final moment and says, "Muy bien!"

Tio Ismael has a son, Samuel, who's about my age. On one of the first few days in Yahualica, Samuel asks me what's going on in the United States. Just under a year after the 2016 presidential election, the only answer I have to offer is first a headshake, then an apologetic shrug, and finally I lower my head. I hope it translates; I don't have the language to talk through it. Also, I'm a bit taken aback. This is the first time I've ever been a representative of the United States. To Samuel, I am unequivocally American. I'm not sure how to feel about it, but I continue nodding in agreement with him. He explains that usually on the Fourth of July, people in the pueblo light fireworks as if celebrating alongside the United States. "This year," he says, "they didn't." I nod again, sorry on behalf of my country, and suddenly the thought that Mexico might never be mine, might never have been mine, floats next to me.

Okay, fine. So I go to Taco Truck for lunch. It's a Tuesday afternoon. There isn't much of a line, but the lunch rush has started. At the window, I order two tacos, and an Agua de Jamaica to drink. The ten-year-old white boy taking my order turns back to the man—who I learn is his father—working the grill to ask if Jamaica is the same as hibiscus tea. Not even turning around, he tells his son, "Jamaica is Spanish for hibiscus—you should learn that." I pay, step aside, and wait for my number to be called.

In Yahualica, after a week at my tio's, my tia Manuela asks if I miss home. The next day she buys me a hamburger and fries from a small restaurant down the street. The day after that she makes spaghetti. I don't know how to explain in a language I can't grasp as well as I wish that I came here for whatever they had to offer, that there isn't anything I need them to change.

Muy bien!

I get the sense that wherever I go in Mexico, my physical presence disrupts time, breaks it apart, all while still trying to wedge itself into place as if, through interaction, an unfortunate mosaic is made. Cracks between each piece are misunderstandings—what doesn't translate or what I don't know how to answer sufficiently. *What's going on with the United States? Are you tired of this food?* Silences that become small channels I slip through before the next moment of noise and voice releases me.

There's no other way to say it: Taco Truck's food is good. I mean, it's fine. It's as good a place to eat as any other "authentic" Mexican spot in Mankato. It has something to do, I think, with nostalgia and expectations set so low based on my skepticism for white midwestern taste buds that actually makes the experience a pleasant one. Would I come back? Sure, maybe.

As I arrived, I depart. The same cab driver comes for me in the morning. A couple photos with my tio's family before I go. The final hugs.

Outside, they wave as the cab pulls away. *Goodbye, el hijo de Juan. Goodbye, el primo del norte.*

On the highway the driver points out a prison in the distance from which El Chapo once escaped. He says something about how everyone was happy. Is this what he thinks I want to hear? *Is it* what I want to hear?

I thought I would leave Minnesota right after I finished a three-year master's of fine arts program. More specifically, I'd envisioned the week after graduation, how my truck would be packed with everything I brought when I first arrived. All the boxes re-taped and stacked. Nothing new, nothing coming back with me from Minnesota. Apartment keys on the kitchen counter, locking the door behind me. One day, I'd just go home. In my truck heading west, trail mix and a frozen water bottle in the seat next to me.

Maybe my problem with Mexican anything in Minnesota is that its proclaimed authenticity relies on stereotype, on what the viewer, those with power, determines. Someone else is having a say at what and how I can be.

Sharon Patricia Holland introduces her book *The Erotic Life of Racism* with a memory from her time living in California. It was the nineties, the week of Tupac's killing. Holland (a Black woman) and her friend's daughter were sitting in a grocery store parking lot talking about his death as they listened to his songs on the radio. Just then, a white woman approached, asking Holland to move her car so that the woman could put her own groceries away. Holland told the woman she'd wait until the woman was finished. In the car Holland and her friend's daughter continued talking, continued listening to music. The woman finished, and when Holland and the girl got out of the car, the writer notes: "What happened next has stayed with me as one of the defining moments in my life in Northern California. As we passed the right rear bumper of her car, she said with mustered indignation, 'And to think I marched for you!'" Holland goes on to say: "The psychic violation of that moment in the parking lot haunts me still; but it is the intimacy of that moment that arrests me. *That woman* expected something *from me*—one usually does not expect anything from a stranger" (1–3).

I'm thinking of the woman from the photo in Mexico City and how "frame" comes from the Old English *framian*, meaning "to be helpful," and *fremman*, "to help forward." Which is not to say the elderly woman selling cups of roasted corn wanted to help me forward, but in *my* photographing of *her*, I believed *she* could be of help to *me*. I wanted a photo of an authentic Mexican, which would support, somehow, a campaign for my own Mexican-ness—which is also a way to resist a type of loneliness—and the idea that in Mexico, I was home. I, the peculiar tourist, finally embraced through photographic evidence: the foreign-made-familiar.

Of the altercation in the grocery store parking lot, Holland says: "that woman ... wanted a connection with me—one solidified through time and place by history, a genealogy that she could readily attach me to" (Holland, *The Erotic Life of Racism*, 5).

But when the Mexican woman stood up from her work and escaped the frame to yell, what did her existence tell me about my own existence? And in Guadalajara, when I'd created a routine, when I went on morning runs, what did I notice besides locals hurrying toward the subway platform or teenagers skating at the park? The other tourists, looking around, hoping to witness something authentic.

"... what happens when someone who exists in time meets someone who only occupies space? Those who order the world, who are world-making master time—those animals *and* humans who are perceived as having no world-making effects—merely occupy space. ... If the black appears as the antithesis (occupies space), the white represents the industry of progressiveness (being in time). It is possible to surmise that resistance to this binary might actually be telling the truth about our sense of time and space instead of a truth about the meeting itself.

"In that moment in the parking lot I was occupying space; the woman was not only occupying time but also performing

her ability to represent its material nature. My temporal imma-
teriality yoked my presence to the needs and desires of my white
female counterpart; my inability to serve therefore represented
an intrusion upon the woman's daily activities. I became an af-
front to *the order of things*, and her comment 'to think I marched
for you' was an invitation to take my place among the officially
sanctioned table of contents for black/white herstory relation"
(Holland, *The Erotic Life of Racism*, 10).

On a Saturday in 2013, three months after moving to Minnesota,
I'm sitting at a long table which is actually just three regular
tables pushed together by workers at the El Mazatlan Mexican
Restaurant. It's the first time so many of the people from my master's program are out together. There's me and about twelve white
people looking through menus. The only other people of color are
the Latinx servers channeling through the restaurant, carrying
trays of food and drinks.

There's this feeling I can't ignore, that I too am part of someone else's authentic Mexican experience, that my existence is
being sucked into another time, another frame of reference, cap-
tured there. Not erasure exactly, but a dwindling of self.

What I know is I'm Mexican. What I know is I'm American.
What I know that day, what is familiar to me, are the voices of
men and women who work in the restaurant, who pick up empty
glasses and drop off sizzling platters, warning people not to
touch. I hear the servers speak to each other between tables. They
sound like my father, my tios, my neighbors back in California.

If this is someone's mini vacation, what role do I play? What
service do I provide? My cracked and glued-in mosaic self. Muy
bien. Just then, one of our waiters shows up on my left with a
notepad and pencil. For a second, when he asks what I'd like to
eat, we're framed there together. And what does that image make
us, make *of* us?—if someone's looking, if someone were to take

a photo to document the evening. Strangers? Friends? Nothing? I consider answering him in Spanish, but I haven't decided what to have.

. . . .

Michael Torres was born and brought up in Pomona, California, where he spent his adolescence as a graffiti artist. His debut collection, *An Incomplete List of Names* (Beacon Press, 2020), was selected by Raquel Salas Rivera for the National Poetry Series. Currently, he lives and teaches in southern Minnesota.

Buy Ten Get One Free! An Open Letter to Bánh Mì Wannabes

· · · · · · · · · · · · · · · · ·

Ánh-Hoa Thị Nguyễn

> I love food made by immigrants. Not only is it delicious,
> but it often has all the elements I look for in a recipe:
> simplicity, resourcefulness, frugality. More important to
> me, though: it is often made by those whose voices have
> been overlooked.
>
> —Edward Lee, *Buttermilk Graffiti: A Chef's Journey*
> *to Discover America's New Melting-Pot Cuisine*

To Whom It May Concern:

The first time I had a banh mi that was not a bánh mì, I was thoroughly flabbergasted. I didn't know something like an imitation bánh mì even existed and only made this discovery when the person I was dating at the time—who is now my spouse despite the lapse in judgment I'm about to describe—brought me one as a consolation while I waited for AAA to service my white and rusted 1992 Camry XLE that broke down while we were on our third date.

It was a sticky summer day in 2010, and we were hanging out in the hippie Seward neighborhood in Minneapolis when he found the "banh mi" at the co-op located a block away from where the car was stranded. The car, unreliable and temperamental, so old that the AC didn't work, spontaneously petered out. Instead of being upset by the inconvenience and the false start of our day together, his chill and thoughtful response was to offer to get us some refreshments while we waited.

After a few minutes he came back with a bag full of goodies and the prospect of making a good impression by bringing me something that reflected my Vietnamese heritage. As I said, it was early on in our courtship, so I didn't blame him for his trusting suburban nature in regard to Vietnamese food sold from an "American" establishment, but the sandwich he brought me was far from the bánh mì I had eaten and had come to love while living in the multicultural food oasis of the Bay Area.

I was trying to be kind, since his gesture was so sweet, but it took everything in me to not blurt out, *What the fuck is this?* Instead, I said, "Thanks so much, but I don't think this is a real bánh mì sandwich." While we waited for the tow truck, I schooled him on the genuine nature of a bánh mì. "First of all," I told him, "a bánh mì is not usually refrigerator cold and uses fresh bread that has a thin, crispy crust and a light and airy inside." The sandwich he bought was wrapped in cellophane and made out of a spongy, hoagie-like bread that had no crunch to it whatsoever.[1]

The second sin of this imitation sandwich wasn't the mock duck (did I mention he is vegan?) but the strange-flavored and overly oily "mayo" that the bread was drenched in. I think it also had bean sprouts in it, or something equally bizarre that doesn't usually come in a bánh mì sandwich. Because I was starting to get hangry and hypoglycemic, I took a bite—but couldn't go further. Luckily, to accompany the sandwich he also bought jalapeño-flavored potato chips, which I have a soft spot for, and I was able to make it through the ordeal without biting his head off.

As a refugee, it was hard for me to forgive him for wasting money on something that was so undeniably inedible, but thankfully this was not a nonnegotiable or repeated behavior, and we were able to avert a dating crisis and soon fell in love. After that

---

[1] Moskin, "Food: Building on Layers": "The Vietnamese dedication to excellent, fresh baguettes is total. Using stale bread is the gravest offense a maker of banh mi can commit."

hot and humid afternoon, however, I began to wonder if this odd "banh mi" sandwich was an anomaly or an appropriated foodie trend that was infecting its way into the Twin Cities scene. To my horror it was the latter: the imposter banh mi was becoming a reality in the majority-white and segregated midwestern region I had returned to then, and still reluctantly call "home."

Even though I lived in Oakland for fifteen years and came of age and consciousness in Northern California, I can never really root out my midwestern upbringing. I grew up in St. Paul just off of the intersection of Wheelock Parkway and Nebraska Avenue, up the hill from Arlington Avenue on the border of St. Paul near the suburb of Roseville. As recent refugees from Vietnam in 1975, my family and I were isolated in this quasi-urban, almost suburban neighborhood and were the only Asian people on the block and solely made up the area's Vietnamese "community." For over twenty-five years, my family of nine lived in a crowded, yellow-tiled, two-story, three-bedroom house on the corner with a lilac bush out front. We had little money and lots of determination to survive.

With a nest of growing children to feed, my parents' go-to grocery store became the Cub Foods on County Road B in Maplewood by the Rice Street exit on Highway 36. This is where they bought what I first learned to think of as "French bread." This anti-artisan, long and foamy loaf of soft bread that was called French bread but did not resemble anything a true Parisian would consider "French" was sold individually, suffocating in a clear, plastic bag. As a matter of fact, it is now known as "US French bread," which refers to the loaf shape that is "longer and wider than a traditional baguette and has rounded ends," and is the same sad bread unfortunately still sold in Cub Foods today.[2]

As a Vietnamese kid growing up poor in the post–Vietnam

---

[2] Clark, "Difference Between French & Baguette Bread."

War, Carter-, then Reagan-era Midwest, it was the only French bread I knew. This was the bread my family ate as a treat with cà ri gà, instead of the day-old, sliced white Wonder Bread loaves that my Ba would get from the Wonder Bakery Thrift Shop. This bread supplemented the few American meals my siblings and I ate together, like spaghetti with meat sauce and lasagna; it was the staple I would sometimes use to make simple ruốc sandwiches when there was nothing else already cooked because my parents were both working long hours. This is the substance that sustained my adolescent appetite for assimilation and Steak-umm sandwiches. These childhood memories were triggered when I bit into that faux banh mi in 2010.

So, when I was a child, I never ate bánh mì "sandwiches." Instead, my Mẹ would roast xá xíu or fry chả chiên, but we would eat these home-cooked meat items alone or with rice or bread on the side and not in a sandwich. Not until bakeries like Ala Francaise, which opened in 1985, appeared on University Avenue in St. Paul did I come to learn what Vietnamese bánh mì was and how it was vastly superior to the Americanized and mono-flavored French bread of Cub Foods. It wasn't often, but when Ba had the time to run to a Vietnamese bakery like Ala Francaise or Trung Nam or Saigon Bakery, we basked in the eating of bánh mì instead of American bread and then in the gradual splurge of sandwiches, since it was rare, in Minnesota, to feel substantiated of our Vietnamese-ness.[3]

As refugees or immigrants finding a new home in the United States, it's hard not to think about food in complex and multifaceted ways. When I left Minnesota as a young woman, my own form of migration, food and foods that reminded me of home came to mean something deeper and more profound than just sustenance. As Amy S. Choi mentions in "What Americans Can

---

[3] Ngo, "Trung Nam Bakery."

Learn from Other Food Cultures," food preferences are person-
ally and culturally meaningful. It is usually one of the last things
people let go of as they assimilate into their new worlds, especially if that new world's dominant culture is white and you are
not. In her article Choi notes that "food is particularly important
when you become part of a diaspora, separated from your mother
culture," and includes these insights from Jennifer Berg, direc-
tor of graduate food studies at New York University: "It's the last
vestige of culture that people shed. . . . There are some aspects
of maternal culture that you'll lose right away. . . . With food, it's
something you are engaged in hopefully three times a day, and so
there are more opportunities to connect to memory and family
and place. It's the hardest to give up."

When I think about my parents and all of the things they
had to give up when they left Vietnam abruptly at the end of the
war—their families, their friends, and everything they knew as
"normal" and "familiar"—I think about all the ways their poor
bodies must have suffered and what they hungered for, things
like home-cooked food from their homeland, to help them feel
human and safe. No wonder so many post-1975 Vietnamese refugees migrated to the area in Southern California called "Little
Saigon" in Orange County so that they could live in a community
that reminded them of home, an actual place where they could
talk and eat with their native tongues.

In the introduction to *The Little Saigon Cookbook*, Ann Le has
this to say about finding authentic Vietnamese cuisine in Little
Saigon: "Here lies a spectacular enclave, built by extraordinary
immigrants who started with virtually nothing. Today, in an
area of roughly 3 square miles, Little Saigon is home to more than
4,000 Vietnamese American businesses and 200 restaurants—
and the largest population of Vietnamese outside of Vietnam."

Areas like these, such as Garden Grove, San Jose, New Orleans, and Houston, gave birth to the diasporic bánh mì—created
and evolved by bánh mì shops sustained with the steam of sweat

by generations of family members, serving their bánh mì filled with fresh ingenuity and hope. This bánh mì, recently deemed by Vietnamese American writer Andrew Lam as "an international sandwich sensation, a culinary wonder of our globalized age," was for first and second waves of refugees another vessel, another boat to venture on, toward their Vietnamese dreams of freedom.

Ba would sometimes allude to his desire to move to this Saigon-away-from-home mecca, but with seven kids, no college degree, and a limited pension, it was never more than an aspiration. Even after his forced retirement, he still talked about wanting to live in a modest mobile home near Little Saigon, just for him and Mẹ to live out their days far from the freezing Midwest.

In 2006, when Ba passed away, Mẹ decided to finally go back to Vietnam after refusing to go for years after the United States lifted its embargo in 1994. She hadn't seen her sisters or her entire extended family, who stayed in Vietnam after the war, for thirty-two years. My oldest sister and I, who were visiting our birthplace for the first time, accompanied her on this homecoming in the winter of 2007. Although I had eaten plenty of delicious Vietnamese food in the Bay Area, this was my first opportunity to taste food that was considered traditionally Vietnamese. What we ate at the Lan Lan 2 Hotel in its splendid breakfast buffet was a spread of some of the tastiest Vietnamese food I have ever eaten, and the warm, fluffy crispiness of fresh-baked bánh mì truly blew my mind. But the simple dishes my aunt cooked for us in her kitchen in Saigon during our family visits reminded me so much of the flavors of Mẹ's kitchen that I almost cried after the first bite.

A decade later I found these tastes of a familiarity that I experienced so viscerally in Vietnam, tastes that were supposed to feel "foreign" to my Americanized tongue but didn't, articulated in Soleil Ho's article titled "Why Is Vietnamese Food in America Frozen in the 1970s?" Ho writes so eloquently, "the enduring image I have of Vietnamese food is only what my parents and grandparents could piece together in their own kitchens. My grandparents and their children cook what is nostalgic for them; in turn, their memories of the past are what I myself crave." After reading her story, I understood the piercing longing that was at the heart of Mẹ's cooking, and that this loss, this emotional haunting, was the same unnamable spice that heated my passion for Vietnamese cuisine and my desire to inherit her culinary knowledge.

Over the years, and especially during these COVID-19 months in quarantine, I've spent more time cooking with Mẹ. One surprising fact I learned about my mother's cooking, only just recently during our lessons, is that she did not learn to cook many of the dishes I grew up eating during her time living in Vietnam. I always assumed that, as the oldest daughter, she learned to cook from her mother, my bà ngoại, who must have been taught by her mother. Instead of having acquired a matrilineal and generational knowledge of cooking through passed-down recipes, Mẹ mastered her culinary skills and her impeccable palate "on the job" during her twenty-seven years as a professional cook in Vietnamese restaurants in the Twin Cities.

As Mẹ gets older and no longer has long days of physical labor in a restaurant or bickering with Ba to distract her, it's harder for her to forget how difficult life was for her back in Vietnam. When she was growing up in Hung Yên in North Vietnam, her family was extremely poor, having endured Japanese occupation in World War II and then the French during the Indochina War. Even after she migrated south to Saigon in 1954 and was later married in 1964 to Ba, she was still poor because eventually they had seven small mouths to feed during yet another war. That's why she never ate complicated or fancy food, and not much meat, and had never eaten a traditional bánh mì thịt nguội or bowl of phở on the street or in a restaurant before coming to the United

States.[4] Her only recollection of eating bánh mì in Vietnam was buying loaves of plain bread from the stall down the street from her home and eating it only at breakfast.[5]

This story made me realize, despite this recent global obsession with phở and bánh mì, how little people really know about Vietnam's past and the class issues and economic conditions that existed before, and especially after, the War in Vietnam and Southeast Asia. As I became more curious about the stories that my mother has only begun to share with me about her life in Vietnam before coming to the United States, I started to become more intense and critical about my research into the history of the country and also its cuisine.

In preparing for this essay, I learned that bánh mì and the baking of it have always been a complicated commixture of class and culture. The tragedy is that most people—especially those who exploit the beauty of bánh mì for trendiness and commercial gain and those who romanticize the French influence on Vietnamese cuisine without acknowledging the "slave-like conditions that the Vietnamese endured on plantations growing opium and rubber" and as forced labor and peasants who farmed land but were not allowed to share in its crops—yes, most people do not know the grim realities of French colonialism (1862–1954) or the history of bánh mì, a history that is filled with as much hypocrisy and contradiction as it is with cooked meat and fresh vegetables.[6]

---

[4] The traditional bánh mì thịt nguội, sometimes called Dặc Biệt (Special or Combination), but also known at Lee's Sandwiches as #1 LEE'S COMBINATION that includes: jambon, headcheese and pâté, house pickle (daikon and carrot), onion, jalapeño, cilantro, salt and pepper, soy sauce, and house mayonnaise. Menu, Lee's Sandwiches.

[5] Thời Đại, "Travel: Banh Mi: 5 Things": "Banh mi is typically eaten at breakfast, usually considered too dry for dinner but is often also eaten as a light snack."

[6] Thời Đại, "Lifestyle: Story of the Banh Mi"; Duiker and Turley, et al., "Vietnam: Effects of French Colonial Rule"; Lion Brand, "History and Origins of Banh Mi."

In *Rice and Baguette: A History of Food in Vietnam*, Vu Hong Lien tells the story of how, at the beginning of French rule in 1884, many of the first colonists were single men who left their families behind in France and therefore were forced to hire local cooks. These cooks were trained to prepare for them "properly cooked French food," and since the most important "authentically" French food that these colonists craved was bread, first called bánh tây (French bread), it was imperative that their subjects learn to perfect its baking. Since "bread making was hot, hard work—too hard for Europeans in the tropical colonies," they trained local workers "to do the drudgery: the mixing, kneading, and baking [of] a never-ending supply of bread."[7]

Although this grueling training laid the foundation for the baking skills that generations of Vietnamese would later carry with them as refugees all over the globe, the people baking bread during the early colonial days were not allowed to eat it because French food was supposed to be consumed only by the French, with the exception of wealthy Vietnamese and Chinese. French baguettes were also very expensive because wheat, not grown in Vietnam, was imported from France, Australia, or the United States, and the race of the baker (often Vietnamese or Chinese) and the percentage of wheat that was used and where it came from affected the reputability of the boulangerie and the authenticity and cost of the bread.[8]

As Erica J. Peters writes in her book *Appetites and Aspirations in Vietnam: Food and Drink in the Long Nineteenth Century*, "people in France ate rice, in risottos, rice puddings, and even with curry. But rice was the primary staple for the Vietnamese; thus, in Vietnam, not eating rice—or claiming not to eat rice—became a way to differentiate oneself from the Vietnamese."

---

[7] Vu, *Rice and Baguette*, 121; Peters, *Appetites and Aspirations*, 157.
[8] Peters, *Appetites and Aspirations*, 157–58.

Therefore, bread making became even more important in Vietnam so that the French could avoid becoming indigenized and continue consuming bread; they further asserted their authority and whiteness over the Vietnamese by also denying them the right to eat bread.[9]

In 1914, at the start of First World War, the two largest import companies in Indochina, the German-owned Speidel & Co. and F. Engler & Co., were seized by the French colonial authorities and their European goods stockpiled. When the French left to assist in the war effort back home, French goods like butter, pâté, charcuterie, and Swiss-made Maggi seasoning became affordable and accessible to working-class Vietnamese. This chance opportunity to consume Western commodities altered food culture in Vietnam and was the catalyst of the Vietnamese appreciation for French foods. The Vietnamese later adapted the French baguette by adding rice flour to account for the humidity and to develop a lighter texture, and these adjustments combined with exposure to those French goods contributed to the creation of the modern-day bánh mì.

As Simon Stanley writes in "The Sandwich That Ate the World," "In the years between the First and Second World Wars, bread became more common in the Vietnamese diet. The French casse croute became the Vietnamese *cát-cụt*." Casse-croûte, I have come to learn, is the French term for "snack" or a way to eat "without really caring about one's table manners whatsoever and includes using your fingers." The Vietnamese and their cát-cụt transformed the traditional way the French consumed their bread, cheese, and charcuterie, which usually came separate on a plate to be eaten as individual items, into the bánh mì sandwich. And as the sandwich moved south to Saigon from Hanoi, other ingredients, like fresh herbs, sauce, or chili, were added and the

---

[9] Peters, *Appetites and Aspirations*, 161.

variations of fillings expanded beyond the traditional pâté and charcuterie that the Vietnamese also learned to make during French colonization.[10]

No one knows for certain the exact year of the birth of the bánh mì, but it was not until the 1950s that bánh mì stalls started to appear on the streets of Vietnam. Although bánh mì was becoming a national sensation, eating it was still heavily associated with class. According to Vu, "By the time the French left Vietnam, two distinct kinds of bánh mì were available, the posh and the stall types. . . . Needless to say the version of posh bánh mì was more expensive and a status symbol for many Vietnamese." For most Vietnamese the stall version was just fine if not better for its versatility and more creative combinations. I like to think this stall bánh mì and the liberation of Vietnam from French rule share a common trajectory of unifying, for at least a short time, the country and the yin and yang characteristics of its diverse, regional cuisines.[11]

Despite my recent surge of research about bánh mì, my real Vietnamese food education began in 1994 when I moved away to California for college. Little did I know that my search for a Vietnamese community out west would lead me to obsessively hunt the Bay Area, and later the country and the world, for the yummiest Vietnamese food I could get my hands on. Having grown up in a latchkey, mostly English-speaking home and white, midwestern bubble, I didn't know then that bánh mì, which simply means "wheat bread" in Vietnamese, was the term synonymous not just with bread but also with a numerous and diverse array of affordable and convenient sandwiches filled with a variety of meats, cold cuts, and pâté, fresh cucumbers and cilantro, pickled carrots and

---

[10] L' Auberge "Chez Richard," "Breaking Bread the French Way."
[11] Vu, *Rice and Baguette*, 129.

daikon, mayo and/or butter, and the ubiquitous Maggi seasoning sauce. (Some Vietnamese delis and bánh mì shops across the country have over twenty different versions on their menus!)

I didn't even realize that I really loved bánh mì until years later, when I started to eat them for lunch on a regular basis at a Vietnamese deli in downtown Oakland's Chinatown called Cam Huong Café, which, like Ala Francaise in St. Paul, has been in operation since 1985. I was a picky eater as a kid, and my favorite bánh mì then and still consists of Chinese-style five-spice barbecue pork (xá xíu) with no pâté, no pickled vegetables, no mayonnaise, and extra cucumber, cilantro, and jalapeño peppers. (I do add crushed red peppers and Maggi, though.) Now I'll branch out to the chả lụa because I can't seem to find amazing xá xíu in the Twin Cities and because it reminds me of the bánh mì that my aunt bought me for breakfast the last time I visited her in Saigon—made with adorable baby bánh mì rolls and heated on the spot in a tiny toaster oven at a street-side cart.

When I was a struggling graduate student, and even after becoming a youngish professional in 2005, since I had huge student loans and lived in the Bay Area, where the rents were rising even as the economy was beginning to recess, bánh mì was one of the foods I could afford to eat "out" for lunch. I didn't realize then that in the late sixties and early seventies in Vietnam, when workers were no longer allowed to go home for a long lunch (two and a half hours!), bánh mì also became a lunchtime snack. Like these Vietnamese before me, I enjoyed bánh mì for lunch because even though it wasn't a hot meal with rice, which I also preferred, at least it was usually toasted and consistently tasty. The truth is, bánh mì "was and is a food staple of the working markets in Vietnam way before it became a fashionable, cheap and hearty dish available to the masses."[12]

---

[12] Vu, *Rice and Baguette*, 131; Thời Đại, "Travel: Banh Mi: 5 Things."

The heartiness of this staple bánh mì is what made the voyage to the United States and what was cultivated in the early eighties by Vietnamese delis and shops that in turn fed countless poor refugee families during their early years here. Even bánh mì expert Andrea Nguyen recalls in her famous book *The Banh Mi Handbook: Recipes for Crazy-Delicious Vietnamese Sandwiches* that as a child her family would buy bánh mì on the weekends in Southern California's Little Saigon, tracking the deals like "three banh mi for $4!" Many of my Vietnamese friends have similar memories of these bánh mì deals from their growing-up years and still say they won't even buy bánh mì from a food establishment not owned by Vietnamese. My favorite bánh mì is at Dong Phuong Bakery in New Orleans, where you can "Buy 10 and Get 1 Free." Although this deal isn't as much of a steal as the buy three get one free, their bánh mì, with spicy red sauce and spectacular bread, is so ridiculously good I would drive eighteen hours during a pandemic to eat one.

The culinary irony, however, is that even though Dong Phuong Bakery is so outstanding it won a James Beard Foundation "America's Classics Award" in 2018, it has been in business since 1982. Why did it take so long for bánh mì to become known to the culinary elite when Vietnamese cuisine has been available in the United States for over forty years? How long does it take for a diaspora to become part of the dominant culture, especially when certain foods are celebrated but their culture and history are not? At what point do Vietnamese, our people and our food, become "American"? Is this lack of reciprocity—reminiscent of the French, who so absolutely refused to adopt Vietnamese cuisine into their own that even today when you Google "Vietnamese influence on French cuisine" you only get search results for "French influence on Vietnamese cuisine"—due to America's inability to reconcile its atrocities and failures during the war in Vietnam?

Why is it that people in the United States still think of Vietnam as a war and not a country of civilians or a complex culture that has given them their precious phở and bánh mì?[13]

Why is it that food service is still one of the few industries in which those who are limited in their choice of profession due to racism and xenophobia and class and cultural barriers and especially those without formal education, citizenship, or English language ability can get hired and make a living? Refugees like my mother, who are never recognized for their labor even though she, and others like her, slaved over hot stoves to cook for thousands of people over the years. These people are the invisible labor that make the food that allows, more often than not, white celebrity chefs to receive accolades and awards and hipster eateries to profit from their overpriced, gentrified versions of other culture's cuisines.

Ten years later, after my first unfortunate "banh mi" incident, non-Vietnamese chefs still put their "interpreted" bánh mì on their menus and act as if they discovered it and bougie co-ops still co-opt them. Vietnamese people have always known that their food is the bomb—we don't need whiteness coming in like Leif Erikson claiming to discover America.[14] Some of us have long known the delicious nature of a bánh mì and the unique joy of hearing the crinkle of the parchment paper it's wrapped in, especially when your mother pulls one out of her purse immediately after she's stepped off the plane from California. Or feeling the crunchy delight when she slips one or two into your cramped carry-on so you have something to eat on your journey. Or when

---

[13] Although Merriam-Webster notes the "First Known Use of banh mi, 1985," bánh mì did not enter culinary reference materials like *The Deluxe Food Lover's Companion* until their 2009 and 2015 editions.

[14] Norse explorer Leif Erikson has been credited with reaching North America five hundred years before Columbus: Weiner, "Coming to America: Who Was First?"; Strass, "Christopher Columbus: 3 Things You Think He Did that He Didn't"; Waxman, "The Troubling History of the Fight to Honor Leif Erikson."

a stranger in Vietnam hands you one on a train because she is worried about you traveling as a woman alone.

For Vietnamese the bánh mì is an extension of our love to eat but also of our need to feed the ones we love. It is a physical and metaphorical bridge; for example, I hand you a part of my culture and you receive and appreciate it, and we have a conversation with and through the sharing of bánh mì. During an interview on the *Racist Sandwich* podcast episode "Tasting Something Other Than Shame," Ijeoma Oluo asserts succinctly that "food is such a fundamental part of our life, and it matters. It's a source of joy; it's a source of connection. In the end we will die without it. And it reaffirms our humanity."

This sense of humanity was reaffirmed for me when I asked my beloved friend TC, who is African American, born and raised in South Side Chicago, two generations removed from Mississippi, about her first experience with bánh mì. She told me that the simple combination of bread and meat reminded her of growing up poor in Chicago, when back in the day it was comforting just to eat a smear of grease on a piece of bread. This empathic remembering opened up the space for us to share stories of our childhoods and to discover how much we had in common—me as a poor Vietnamese refugee and her as a poor Black girl just trying to make it through.

It is this resilience and instinct to survive that is quintessentially Vietnamese, yet shared with other Black, Indigenous, and People of Color communities, that I think of when I hunger for a bánh mì. To me, bánh mì is not only a sandwich but also a symbol of ultimate sacrifice—of lives lost in multiple attempts of escape, of certainty for uncertainty on a foreign shore, of sixteen-hour workdays and multiple jobs and parents never getting to spend time with their children, of losing one's culture for the success of assimilation, of individual satisfaction for family security, and of sending money desperately needed in the United States back home to family in other countries. The stinging sacrifice of not being able to feed home-cooked meals to your loved ones for the serving and selling of store-cooked meals to strangers.

This resourcefulness endured and mastered by my diaspora is the special sauce I taste when I eat bánh mì: an addictive balance of bittersweet saltiness and spice, simple yet scrumptiously supreme layering of flavors, that generations after generations of refugees and immigrants intuitively recognize and savor.

Do you know what that tastes like?

Yours truly,
Ánh-Hoa Thị Nguyễn

. . . .

Ánh-Hoa Thị Nguyễn is a poet, community artist and curator, educator, and gastronome. She holds an MFA in creative writing from Mills College in Oakland, California, where she discovered her affinity and love for finding fresh produce and feeding friends. Ánh-Hoa is also a book artist, cocktail creator, and cookbook enthusiast.

Bibliography

Cambridge Dictionary. casse-croûte. https://dictionary.cambridge
　　.org/dictionary/french-english/casse-croute.
Cam Huong Café-Deli-Restaurant. http://www.camhuong.com.
Choi, Amy S. "What Americans Can Learn from Other Food Cul-
　　tures." Ideas.Ted.com, December 18, 2014. https://ideas.ted.com/
　　what-americans-can-learn-from-other-food-cultures.
Clark, Sara. "Difference Between French & Baguette Bread." eHow,
　　Leaf Group Ltd., August 30, 2017. https://www.ehow.com/
　　info_8484946_difference-between-french-baguette-bread.html.
Dong Phuong Banh Mi and Baked Goods. Menu: Bake Shop: Banh Mi.
　　https://www.dpbakeshop.com/DP-Bakeshop-Menu.pdf#page2.

Duiker, William J., and William S. Turley, et al. "Vietnam: Effects of French Colonial Rule." Encyclopædia Britannica, Inc., March 17, 2020. https://www.britannica.com/place/Vietnam/ Effects-of-French-colonial-rule.

Ho, Soleil. "Why Is Vietnamese Food in America Frozen in the 1970s?" TASTE, November 20, 2018. https://www.tastecooking.com/ vietnamese-food-america-frozen-1970s.

JBF Editors. "Introducing the 2018 America's Classics Winners." James Beard Foundation, January 18, 2018. https://www.jamesbeard.org/ blog/introducing-the-2018-americas-classics-winners.

Lam, Andrew. "Bánh Mì: The Rise of the Vietnamese Sandwich." *HuffPost*, July 14, 2015; updated December 6, 2017. https://www .huffpost.com/entry/banh-mi-the-rise-of-the-v_b_7794840.

L' Auberge "Chez Richard." "Breaking Bread the French Way: Casse-croûte." Auberge Chez Richard, February 2, 2010. https:// aubergechezrichard.blogspot.com/2010/02/breaking-crust -french-way.html.

Le, Ann. *The Little Saigon Cookbook: Vietnamese Cuisine and Culture in Southern California's Little Saigon*. 2006. Reprint: Guilford, CT: Globe Pequot Press, 2011.

Lee, Edward. *Buttermilk Graffiti: A Chef's Journey to Discover America's New Melting-Pot Cuisine*. New York: Artisan, a Division of Workman Publishing, 2018.

Lee's Sandwiches. Menu: Asian Sandwiches. https://leesandwiches .com/menu/1-lees-combination/.

Lion Brand. "The History and Origins of Banh Mi." *Lion Pride: The Official Lion Brand Blog*, February 23, 2018. http://www.lionbrand .com.au/blog/the-history-and-origins-of-banh-mi.

Merriam-Webster Dictionary. "banh mi." https://www.merriam -webster.com/dictionary/banh%20mi.

Moskin, Julia. "Food: Building on Layers of Tradition." *New York Times*, April 7, 2009. https://www.nytimes.com/2009/04/08/ dining/08banh.html.

Ngo, Nancy. "Trung Nam Bakery's Owner Talks about His Fluffy, Flaky Croissants and Baguettes." *Twin Cities Pioneer Press*, July 17, 2017; updated July 18, 2017. https://www.twincities .com/2017/07/17/trung-nam-bakerys-owner-talks-about -his-fluffy-flaky-croissants-and-baguettes.

Nguyen, Andrea Quynhgiao. *The Banh Mi Handbook: Recipes for Crazy-Delicious Vietnamese Sandwiches.* Berkeley, CA: Ten Speed Press, 2014.

Nguyễn Đình Hoà. *Vietnamese-English Student's Dictionary.* Saigon: Vietnamese American Association, 1967.

Oluo, Ijeoma. "E52: Tasting Something Other Than Shame (w/Ijeoma Oluo)." *Racist Sandwich,* July 14, 2018. http://www.racistsandwich.com/episodes/2018/6/26/e52-tasting-something-other-than-shame-w-ijeoma-oluo.

Peters, Erica J. *Appetites and Aspirations in Vietnam: Food and Drink in the Long Nineteenth Century.* Lanham, MD: AltaMira Press, 2012.

Stanley, Simon. "The Sandwich That Ate the World." *Roads & Kingdoms,* June 21, 2016. https://roadsandkingdoms.com/2016/the-sandwich-that-ate-the-world.

Strauss, Valerie. "Christopher Columbus: 3 Things You Think He Did That He Didn't." *Washington Post,* October 14, 2013.

Thời Đại, Vietnam Times: The Vietnam Union of Friendship Organizations. "Lifestyle: Story of the Banh Mi: Vietnam's Super Sandwich that Took on the World." October 29, 2019. https://vietnamtimes.org.vn/story-of-the-banh-mi-vietnams-super-sandwich-that-took-on-the-world-16774.html.

Thời Đại, Vietnam Times: The Vietnam Union of Friendship Organizations. "Travel: Banh Mi: 5 Things You Might Not Know about Vietnamese Sandwich." March 26, 2020. https://vietnamtimes.org.vn/banh-mi-5-things-you-might-not-know-about-vietnamese-sandwich-18761.html.

Vu, Hong Lien. *Rice and Baguette: A History of Food in Vietnam.* Food and Nations Series. London: Reaktion Books, 2016.

Waxman, Olivia B. "The Troubling History of the Fight to Honor Leif Erikson—Not Columbus—as the Man Who 'Discovered America.'" *Time,* October 4, 2019. https://time.com/5414518/columbus-day-leif-erikson-day.

Weiner, Eric. "Coming to America: Who Was First?" National Public Radio, Books, October 8, 2007. https://www.npr.org/templates/story/story.php?storyId=15040888.

The Measurements
· · · · · · · · · · · · · · · · ·
V. V. Ganeshananthan

I went to learn about the war.

I wanted to learn exactly what it was, but no one could tell me. Some people did not want to tell me, and others knew they could not. If you don't know which war I mean, wait: I'll tell you. Or, better: you can figure it out.

Often, the person telling me about the war ate as they talked. Sometimes, when I was younger, I listened so quietly they barely knew I was there. Later, sometimes I cooked for them; sometimes they cooked for me; sometimes, if we were both activists, we cooked and talked about politics together until we knew each other well enough for whatever was necessary next.

Eating is an intimacy. This is why when one Sri Lankan politician betrayed the other, people learning the story repeated to each other in astonished tones: they had just eaten appam together. That morning.

I grew up in the 1980s, in the middle of potlucks and dinner parties, as people discussed the war. Do you know which one I mean yet? Up and down the East Coast of my childhood, the talkers talked and ate off of those Styrofoam plates with little compartments that keep your curries segregated. Who wanted their curries segregated? I don't know. Some of the talkers, even those related to each other, and sometimes especially those related to each other, did not agree about the war. Some of them learned to avoid talking about disagreeable subjects. Others learned to agree. Others eventually stopped coming to the potlucks and dinner parties and temples and celebratory and ethnic functions. The children ate too, and listened. We drank soda—orange soda, Coke, Sprite, or 7 Up—out of Styrofoam cups. We crushed the plates and cups without knowing that they were bad for the planet; we slid them into trash cans, hoping that our mothers (or even other people's mothers, who in those close quarters minded our business too) did not notice if we failed to eat everything they had put on our plates.

Will you consume the story you were given? Will you wait for more? Do you know what went into your food? In what amounts? What it cost? Or did you eat what appeared without thinking? I did.

After we ate, the children waited for dessert. We wished for something easy and sweet. When it came—ice cream and wattalappam and pineapple fluff, which if you have not eaten it has an appeal akin to how I imagine Narnian Turkish delight—we ate it and listened.

My knife skills come from sous-chefing for my mother, who learned to cook after emigrating. She never taught me how to cook anything, not with exact measurements, and not with any exact amounts of time. Just watch, she said. Are you watching? Perhaps she was a little impatient with my desire for exactitude and my desire to be told. If you watch carefully, she said, you will see how it is made, what exactly is going on. You taste the curry as you are cooking by tapping it into the fleshiest part of your palm, below your thumb. Nothing will burn you there. Are you surprised? Haven't you seen me do this a thousand times?

My parents took us to a Sri Lankan restaurant in New York City. We had never been to the restaurant before, but my father nodded at a man at another table. He nodded back. Who is that? I asked him. I know him, my father said; the Tigers killed his brother a few years ago. I remembered the story. The candlelight in the restaurant flickered. Years passed before I learned that the Sri Lankan ambassador, too, liked to eat there. I wondered which sets of politics crossed paths over plates.

My brother moved to New York City. He found every place where he could get Tamil and Sri Lankan food: the food cart on the south side of Washington Square Park, where a former swim coach from Jaffna came to know us; a restaurant in Curry Hill, so small that the waiters squeezed by us, bumping elbows while serving beautifully molded plates of koththu roti, which originated as a street food; a bare-bones place on Staten Island, where he was not displeased when the store misunderstood his idiappam to-go order as fifty instead of fifteen. Will that be enough, rasa? the woman behind the counter said to my brother. She spoke in Tamil, and said it like he was related to her, and my own mother, visiting, laughed.

My parents grew up eating mostly fish, and chicken only occasionally; in Sri Lanka, that was more affordable. In America, the opposite was true, so I grew up eating chicken curry almost every day. Because as a child I did not like parippu, which my mother made to accompany every dinner, chicken was my main protein. It was probably the first curry I ate as a child; she used to wash the spicy kuzhambu off before mixing it with rice and feeding it to me by hand. When I was old enough to eat the kuzhambu, that became my favorite part; I drowned my rice in it. I gasped as I ate and the afterburn of Jaffna curry powder accumulated. Jaffna curry powder, which is roasted, has perhaps more chilli powder than other curry powders; it is red, not the yellow you would find in most grocery stores. My mother could never tell if I was distressed or happy that her food was so hot.

· · · · · · · · ·

I took a bus to visit my brother in New York. Before I returned, he took me to a Sri Lankan buffet near Port Authority. The maître d' recognized him; we ate voraciously before my return journey. I remember mango pudding. Later still, when I asked my brother to take me back there, he told me the restaurant had burned down and would not be rebuilt.

I first learned to cook chicken curry myself after college, when I roomed with a pal who appreciated good food; he taught me to make chili, and I asserted that I could return the favor by cooking my mother's Jaffna-style chicken curry. He wanted to take me up on it, and could deliver on his end of the bargain easily. But I discovered right away that I had overpromised on my skills; I called my mother, who coached me through the steps. It was a slower dish than some others, I learned, but well worth it.

This also began my habit of calling my mother when I cooked—a habit I later kept, out of sheer stubbornness, even when I knew exactly how to make what I wanted. As I became a better cook myself and video chat became more common, I would show her my progress on FaceTime. Is this meat okay? How much coconut milk? Is the curry too red? Can I really not substitute salsa if I don't have tomatoes and green chillies? (No, you can't. At least once, too lazy to go to the store in an Iowan winter, I did anyway.) She cooked with me over the phone when I lived in Virginia, Iowa, New Hampshire, New York, Michigan, Massachusetts, and Minnesota.

Weren't you watching me cook when you lived with us? she asked.

Yes. No. Show me again.

By the spring of 2009, when the Sri Lankan civil war was ending, I lived in New York City myself, and turned to one dish repeatedly for comfort. Chicken curry is the one Jaffna-style food I can now make without a recipe, without calling my mother, without anyone else. Although for years my mother held my hand virtually, today I can make chicken curry absentmindedly, seamlessly, while talking to a friend or colleague; it is also the one labor-intensive curry I will reliably make for myself even on the kind of day when cooking seems like it might not be worthwhile. The version I know and believe in is one I chose, after comparing many different options. I do not need measurements or a timer or even all the ingredients, since so many are to taste or optional. As an adult, I have made it the alpha and omega of my culinary repertoire—and never more so than that year. Because I know it by heart, it makes any kitchen familiar, too, in the cooking.

I craved this familiarity during the war's final spring, as casualties among Tamil civilians—and the debate over those casualties—mounted. The scale exceeded anything I had seen before; I went from news to work to cooking to analyzing and back again, with little in between. Fortunately, although I made chicken curry alone around that time, I also made it with others. I had become politicized as a graduate student a couple of years before that, through friendships with scholars who studied Sri Lanka, and had developed a habit of making chicken with new friends and collaborators as I learned which parts of the stories of my childhood were wrong or incomplete. Some of the people who told me stories and gave me books were familiar with the roasted Jaffna curry powder I favored, but each family had taught its children the dish with subtle household differences—and beyond that, we had all developed our own individual New York hacks to get around the lack of certain ingredients, and to honor our own preferences. One friend of mine always got his meat fresh, at a halal butcher; one preferred a squeeze of lemon at the end; another layered spices in a very particular order. Some were swift and furious cooks; others paused for long, beery, political dialogues. I watched and filed away things to try, taking careful note of which people made the best dishes. Nobody measured.

· · · · · · · · · ·

Now my way goes like this:

cinnamon stick
pinch fennel seed
pinch cumin seed
pinch fenugreek seed
pinch mustard seed
pinch whole cloves, optional
pinch whole peppercorns, optional
pinch cardamom, optional
curry leaves, torn, optional (but much better with)
ginger
minced garlic (so many cloves!)
1 medium onion, chopped (or more, to taste)
1 green chilli (or more, to taste)
some arbitrary amount of chicken (I usually make what others would
    consider an ill-advised amount because if you freeze the leftovers
    you will feel like a genius later and also the only thing better than
    fresh chicken curry is second-day chicken curry. Use thigh meat.
    Bones are good, but when I am feeling lazy and indulgent I'll use
    boneless and skinless meat—I generally feel lazy and indulgent
    on this count.)
Jaffna curry powder (to taste; start with a little—you can add
    more easily)
salt to taste
1 fresh tomato (or more, to taste)
black pepper to taste
coconut milk

Combine the spices (cinnamon stick through chilli) in a large pot.
Cook, stirring, until the onion is translucent and the spices fragrant.
Add chicken with curry powder and salt. Let it cook for a few minutes,
and then add some water (to taste, depending on how thick you want
your curry) and a chopped tomato, plus pepper, if you want. When it
seems done (the tomato having vanished), turn up the temperature
briefly. Add some coconut milk; wait until it boils. Turn off heat.
Serve hot, with rice. Call your mother.

Around the time the war was ending, a group of diasporic Lankan
leftists convened at a progressive space in New York's West Vil-

lage. A number of us who had corresponded met in person for the first time. Several of us saw a man we thought looked familiar, but none of us could place him. We wondered if he was there to disrupt things, and if so, how. When he stepped to the microphone during the question and answer and opened his mouth to deny the facts the panelists had shared, we gasped collectively: we knew him because he owned the Lankan restaurant we all went to, and which after that day I never went to again.

Six years past the end of the war, within a few weeks of moving to Minnesota in the fall of 2015, I was sick. Maybe I didn't pack the genetics or the antibodies for the Upper Midwest—who knows. Whatever it was, it was nothing that would go away easily. It lasted seven and a half months, and encompassed something like seven consecutive sinus infections and five consecutive upper respiratory infections. I was new to town, and I wanted to show up at every social event I could. The answer to *how are you liking it in Minnesota* was *I kind of can't breathe here*, but that's not a great thing to say when you are trying to make new friends, so I smiled, came home, and collapsed.

Drained from shortness of breath, inflamed sinuses, and a near-constant headache, I didn't care what I ate; I only wanted to sleep. My face hurt. After one stray Minnesota Nice salad (wild rice!), I subsisted, disgustingly, on an array of high-protein yogurts and KIND bars, accompanied by rivers of tea, lakes of honey, forests of ginger, plateaus of peanut butter toast. Chicken curry was a memory. I invented my own makeshift salad, which I dubbed Efficiency Meal—tomato, avocado, chopped-up light string cheese, olive oil, salt, vinegar if I could find it. I spooned soup from, alternately, boxes and cans. If this counted as a cuisine it was probably Low American Processed. Formerly beloved jars of spices stood untouched and musty in the cabinet. I had almost entirely stopped cooking for myself. I felt myself pulsing with preservatives, but didn't have the energy to do better.

Fortunately for me, someone else did. For some years I had been Facebook friends with a fellow Sri Lankan American artist who, it turned out, was extremely friendly and lived only ten minutes away from my new place in Minneapolis. She had immigrated to Illinois from Sri Lanka when she was six, and moved to Minnesota at fifteen. I already knew and admired her art. Come over! she wrote. I wanted to meet her, but I was exhausted. I can't, I wrote back, but thanks for the invite. Come over, she suggested again. I can't, I have work, I responded, but thanks for still inviting me. Come over, she said, and you can say no, but I'm going to keep inviting you until you come. By this point, I was impressed at not only her friendliness but also her persistence. She meant it. Finally, one day when I was done with work and had enough energy left, we met up.

How's it going? she asked. You don't seem well.

I've been a little under the weather, I said.

You can't get better if you don't eat, she said. I'm cooking for my family anyway. You should come over once or twice a week until you get better.

I don't want to trouble you, I said, very much wanting to trouble her.

No trouble, she said. Come over! Come over.

So for months, I went over. Sometimes she picked me up and dropped me off—I had no car, and even the mild Minnesota winter was chilly. Her two small daughters became new little friends, too. Aunty Sugi! they exclaimed. Her husband poured me ill-advised and much-needed whiskies. He is Japanese American, and my friend had developed her own Lankan Japanese fusion: onigiri stuffed with Sri Lankan curries: sambol of coconut and red chilli, or chicken curry. She made Lankan rice and curry meals, too: red rice and varae (or mallung), and squash curry. I loved watching her chop swiftly and efficiently. (I want to be friends with everyone with excellent knife skills.) She invited me to join a regular Sri Lankan potluck of her friends, and took me to restaurants she loved, including a Lankan one. She explained and discussed her recipes. She handed me lunch boxes of leftovers— onigiri in tidy, delicious rows. Her family is Sinhalese, and mine mostly Tamil, so our words for foods were sometimes different, but hers were still familiar.

It was a pleasure to watch her cook, to understand her particularities as a chef, to compare them to my own, to remember that I *had* particularities and had once cared about what I ate, to realize that cooking certain things that I missed might not be as hard as I'd thought, to see that eating with others and eating Lankan food might make me hungry again. I loved that she treated the making of food as another art; it was something I had forgotten how to do, and she gently reminded me. She was so consistently glad to see me, and her friendliness and meals were a stove on which I steadily warmed. Come over, she'd said to me; if we had both been in Sri Lanka, the phrase, I knew, was quite often *come home*.

Come home, by which the sayers meant, I will give you home-cooked food. Come to my house and feel like it is yours.

By mid-spring, I was beginning to recover—I could sprint for a bus again, and walk a flight of stairs without getting winded. I had friends in my new town, and I was beginning to cook again. One year later, I learned to make a dish that both my friend and my mother make: that delicious coconut sambol. Both of them make it better than I do, so when they cook, I watch them closely. Two different ways, both instinctual and delicious.

My best try goes like this:

> Begin by toasting red chillies (six of them, for perhaps eight servings of the sambol as a side dish, but who's measuring?). Put them in a tiny bit of oil (a teaspoon) in a frying pan until they become shiny and heated through. Take the chillies out of the pan and put in shredded, unsweetened coconut, along with chopped red onion to taste, some

ginger chopped finely, curry leaves torn into pieces, and salt (you can add more later, to taste). Warm the coconut in the pan with the other ingredients—you're heating it lightly, not really cooking it. Turn off the stove after the coconut is warmed through.

Put the chillies in a food processor and grind them. Then add the rest of the ingredients from the pan. Grind it through until the coconut turns bright. Add more salt if needed. If you need to increase the spiciness you can add plain red chilli powder into the food processor. Serve alongside rice and curries, with thosai, or with appam. Decide whether the heat is distressing or happy.

These days, my friend and my mother and I sometimes play a game of culinary telephone. My friend tries something new; I taste it or she tells me about it, and as I walk from her place back to mine I describe it to my mother, who is always interested. How does your mother make this other dish? my friend wants to know. Faithfully I relay the question, and cheerfully my mother answers. Precious ingredients, too, change hands. Years ago my mother told me about the many things she and her other Sri Lankan friends taught each other to make after they immigrated to the United States and their childhood kitchens were far away. They could not talk to their mothers as they cooked; they called their friends. How creative they became with substitutes, how generous they were when one of them lucked into the missing vegetable or spice they all wanted. Now, when I visit my parents, my mother goes to her flourishing plants and makes two packets of curry leaves. When I go back to Minnesota, my friend always exclaims with delight at their home-nourished size and freshness, impossible to find in any store.

These days, I live even closer to her, and after so many meals at her house, sometimes it is my turn to cook. What do I feel brave enough to make for someone who has served me such delicious meals, hospitality, and warmth in a place where I still feel new? Minnesota is the tenth state in which I've lived. Here, as anywhere, I can do no better than the food I know by heart, and to which I always return: chicken curry. It is my mother's dish, become mine—still the only one that makes any kitchen familiar in the cooking, and for which I use no measurements.

· · · · · · · · · · · · · · · ·

V. V. Ganeshananthan, a fiction writer and journalist, is the author of *Love Marriage*, a novel set in Sri Lanka and its diaspora communities. The book was longlisted for the Orange Prize and named one of *Washington Post* Book World's Best of 2008. She is the cohost of Literary Hub's *Fiction/Non/Fiction* podcast, which is about the intersection of literature and the news. Excerpts from her second novel, forthcoming from Random House, have appeared in *Granta, Ploughshares,* and *Best American Nonrequired Reading.*

"These Are the Plates of Our Lives"

. . . .

Senah Yeboah-Sampong

In the second half of the year 2020, I came to Mother's south Minneapolis home after my Friday shift in a suburban fulfillment center. As ever, I was caught in transition, dodging in and out of the many tableaus and backdrops I try to blend into, starved for some refuge, in that timeless, familiar, and cosmic sense.

My cousin Jackie was newly engaged, and that night some of us would meet her fiancé for the first time. Once again we celebrated new life, new family, new genesis. *If you know, you know.* There is no party without food, and I was so, so ready.

I found everyone at the table on the first split level, sunlight accenting their rich melanin with a warm, subtle glow; here were my two uncles, Steven and Paul, and my aunt Christine, Paul's wife. My cousins Kenisha and Rachel—Jackie's older sister—were both there. All three of my cousins wore some variation of gold on black. An open box of face masks sat next to the many-headed Ghanaian centerpiece. Our greetings were warm, inquisitive, relaxed, and relaxing. Maybe, for now, we were just glad to see one another healthy and in good spirits, especially with the world on fire.

My mother led me to the spread of pans and dishes on the nearby counter. I smelled rice and beans, sautéed catfish, pork chops, baked chicken. I gave a nod to my mother's lidded salad bowl, ever loaded to the brim with freshness. I plated a blend of old-country diet and new, to digest and reconsider the quintessence of my family. My understanding of that substance is in large part the by-product of a return my mother made to Uganda with me in 2004, the year I miraculously graduated from high school. I, like others, have in many ways starved through rough patches in my life, willingly and unwittingly. At that particular time, my body was the site of chemical and metaphysical experimentation, undertaken in hopes of discovering something real about who I was, what I was made of, and how I would cope with what seemed the bleak specter of adulthood.

Throughout my life, every instance of fasting and gluttony made every crumb my people offered me a tangible manifestation of love and concern for my well-being, even when I was too down and too stubborn to recognize these caring acts for what they were. Investments in my survival have been provided both here in Minneapolis, Minnesota, and in Kampala, Uganda, the motherland of my mothership, and for that I am eternally grateful.

When I arrived in late June 2004, Ugandan cuisine was unfamiliar to me, save for bits and pieces of hard times that hit my plate when my jaajaa, my grandfather, would send my mother care packages full of smoked, seasoned fish and ziplock bags full of whole groundnuts she oven roasted, or the rare plantain or mango she sought out and made a point to share with me.

In the early 1980s my mother, Rachel, was the second of her siblings to arrive in the states after her elder brother, Moses. But while Uncle Moses made his stand in New York City, my mother had made up her mind to set down in Minneapolis. Mom arrived in the winter, she told me, an overwhelming season with which anyone who lives a year in this state becomes well acquainted.

On top of Mom's homesickness, the processed food she ate caused an allergic reaction. She had never used or consumed pesticides, and the concept of preservatives was truly foreign to her body. While I came up eating Chef Boyardee, General Mills, and Kraft products, my mother was sustained on locally grown food. For her, there simply were no other options.

. . . .

She told me that the main staple of her Ugandan diet was matoke, a kind of green banana normally mashed like potatoes, though the process was more complicated than that. *There was lumonde, the white sweet potatoes; cassava* (aka yucca root); *and maize*, basically corn with a much tougher kernel than what I get in the states. *Most of these dishes were accompanied by various sauces, such as groundnut sauce; pea soup; beans; greens (mainly spinach), bitter balls with onions, tomatoes, carrots; tomato stew; beef, dried fish, chicken, pork, to say nothing of the tilapia that came straight out of Lake Ukerewe.*

Every family had a patch of gardens full of fruits and veggies, grown through manual cultivation. Mother told me: *We would just get up and pick food from our backyards for daily consumption. Some folks who did not have food would buy from the market. I do not remember my family buying from the market because we grew plenty of food. My family produced most of the food we ate, except beef or other meat products like fish, pork, goat meat, etc. My father cultivated a lot of fruits, which included pawpaws, mangoes, jackfruit, small sweet bananas, pineapples, oranges. . . . We had plenty of those, and we would sometimes eat those all day before dinner would be ready. It was rare to have breakfast like in the United States. We ate two major meals: lunch and late dinner, like around 8:00 PM. My mother had a flock of goats, but it was rare to have a goat butchered for consumption. Instead, my father would go to the market and buy goat meat or beef.*

For *my* mother then, as for me during my months in Kampala, everything was prepared and eaten the same day, as a common meal for the entire house. There was no reliable refrigeration and so no other choice.

During the six-month gap with my Nsubuga-Masaazi family, I would build relationships with these and other vittles. A part of it, I think, was faith that my people would hold me down, and that I would make do if I wanted to stay alive and healthy. When I traveled with my mother in '04, I tried to consider how the culture shock I experienced mirrored my mother's some twenty years prior, only she didn't have people on the ground who had her back. I imagine now that the whole idea of mass-produced, chemically altered food might've seemed a bit odd to the young woman who arrived here over thirty-five years ago, who worked the Calhoun Beach Club, Metrodome concessions, and Target retail to make rent on an Uptown studio.

In choosing to spend that time with my aunt Rebecca and our family on the Kampala hill and neighborhood called Nakulabye, I was far less clear on my "why," or for how long, than my mom had been in leaving the place. I was just mature enough to recognize that I needed distance, at least for a while, from my old friends, habits, and habitat if I were going to stay sober. I also wanted to feel closer to our family, to be held in community, beyond what seemed an eternal struggle to find economic stability and psychospiritual balance in our whitewashed tundra. I felt all of these things but lacked the language to articulate those thoughts at the time.

Much as I respected and loved my mother, her life, who she was or had been on the continent, was mysterious and intriguing to me. Throughout our lives together—specifically her three years pushing for a Western juris doctorate on full-time hours—my mother's yearning for that psychospiritual balance included the ongoing search for a taste of something familiar. She had no time to relax or to sleep. No one took care of her, outside of taking me off her hands for a few hours or a couple of days. This rough-and-tumble period was when the care packages from Jaajaa came in the mail, at the times they were most needed. What powerful magic: that the matter my mother, her parents, and her grandparents consumed paves my neural networks, muscle fibers, and skin cells and became our bone marrow, our reproductive cells; that someway, somehow, I am made of the African continent.

I still see our small kitchen, in the late nineties, off East Twenty-Eighth Street and Eleventh Avenue, from a perch on the card table, the countertop, or the fridge. On any given Sunday, my mother would blast the radio or one of her cassettes—the *Sarafina!* soundtrack, or maybe Simon & Garfunkel's greatest hits—and get to work on one of the brown bundles she might've stashed for a week or a month in the freezer. It was a tender affair. I see now how preparing food was for my mother what it has become for me: a therapeutic meditation, a caring for the mind and the body, a sacrament to our ancestors, the mercy of the earth herself in the face of so much inhuman cruelty. I can smell the smoked fish, the freeze-dried groundnut paste she mixed with peanut butter to get the consistency right, so savory and rich, full-bodied in flavor with a gravy consistency that didn't jibe with its opacity. I can see her taking her knife to the fish, cutting through to the dry, white insides, crumbling it in her hand to fall into the pot. We sit cross-legged in front of the TV, watching *60 Minutes*, plates on our big area rug. *Watch out for the small bones, Senah. I don't want you to choke!*

After three days dead asleep, my 2004 trip to Uganda began with an empty belly telling me to put in whatever I could, and a knee that jerked at the sight and smell of every covered platter placed before me. Most meals took place in Aunt Becca's or Jaajaa's house, where a goat had been slaughtered and stewed at the end of the two weeks my mom and I had spent there just four years earlier. That visit in 2000 was Mom's first trip back in over twenty years in the United States.

In '04, however, that first breakfast set the tone for all others that followed. It was eggs with gray yolks, from the smaller, leaner chickens that ran around the compound, trailed by lines of chicks, who nested under banana trees cordoned off behind grimy barbed wire. I found that poultry tougher, leaner when it appeared in my soup; it tasted different from what I was used to, urban free-range, I suppose. The eggs were hard-boiled or made into a thick, onion-fried, salted omelet. Either version always included circular slices of tomato and thick slices of buttered bread.

A bowl of pineapple and pawpaw ("po-po"), aka papaya, would usually be served on the side, and perhaps a dilution of passion fruit with a spoonful of raw sugar.

This combination gave me the energy for computer programming classes at Makerere University, a straight shot from the nearest intersection, by taxi or boda boda (motor scooter) or on foot, maybe three-quarters of a mile from my front door. Makerere was my mother's college, where she had gotten her first postsecondary degree and juris doctorate. The school is legendary in the region and on the continent for the scholars it has produced. I was honored to attend and certainly intimidated. If I could at least practice learning, I thought, then this could be good for me. And so it was.

The classes were fine. Time at the compound was everything, though, and the food we shared seemed to metabolize the xenophobia, culture shock, and spatiotemporal displacement that this American life has left me with, setting me to drift through any moment but the present one. The food my family prepared and offered me every day alongside them healed me and helped me begin patching fractures between myself and the people to whom I truly belong.

It was always a pleasure to accompany Aunt Becca to a local open market on one side of the roundabout. This ritual was a romantic foray to collect proteins and the like for main dishes that would last for a day, or three, or a week, depending on who was home and what was available. Inhale and catch the sharp scent of drying blood over diesel exhaust and stale, standing water. Dusty sunlight falls between flimsy steel panels over rows of stalls, those panels providing austere shade from the harsh equatorial sun. I see the hanging scale and stained butcher's block. I hear the lively exchange of barter . . . and gossip, I imagine. I am ashamed to say I did not understand, and would not understand even now.

At the Kampala compound of the early aughts, a lot of the local, manual food cultivation still took place. I can see the small, green-skinned palms, with broad green leaves, wearing long bundles of green matoke. Here is the lumonde bush, spreading tall and wide over a narrow, thin trunk, its branches dropping tendrils back to the soil where the tubers would get big and strong. There stands the strong, orderly jackfruit tree, with broad branches and waxen leaves, loaded down but never bowed by fruits the size of an adult's torso, covered in a seemingly reptilian skin. I see the machete rise and fall against the harvested jackfruit, split now to reveal the stacked rings of seeds, covered in the buttery-sweet flesh of what I proclaimed the "king of fruits." Ah, and there is a stand of sugarcane; oh, thank you, sabo, for cutting and serving up some of *that*, so sweet and refreshing, I chew the pulped fibers until they slice my inner cheek, and keep chewing.

There was the legendary day of two tilapia. Aunt Becca had the day off and bought them from a man up the road to the church. She had then cleaned and gutted them, seasoned them with dry marinade, stuffed them with chopped onion, and spitted them to dry until dinner, when they were fried over a sigiri and served up. So simply prepared, it was so good I wanted to cry.

It took me more than two months to accept the casual care and attention of my cousins. Even the concept of "cousin" had no place here. These were my brothers and sisters, more than I could name, more than I could count. Aunts Deborah and Sarah visited almost daily. My uncles cycled through from the states with their young children, many of whom I had never met—like Kenisha and Rachel, Kendrick, Lillian. There was so much power in just sharing space, feeling their energy wash over and through mine. I sensed, then later understood, that we had all been in fellowship here before, had lived and loved each other here before over the same meals, and that we would again. Yes, we were working on the other side of time now. Perhaps, I thought, I could consider "time as officially ended."

I came to see how my American experience had softened and spoiled me. I didn't have the strength to do my laundry by hand.

It took me many weeks to determine how to turn a bucket of boiling water into a thorough bath. Every morning began with the cock's crow—and the sight of one or another cousin already out and stooped to sweep the paths around the house. Every evening one or more of them would clean the dishes that had been left to soak all day, readying them for the next meal. My family boiled and washed my clothes by hand as necessary. I felt like a baby, but I understood on some level that we were all trying to make up for the lost time.

In the mornings I watched children of all ages leave for school as the sun rose. My aunt Becca, whom everyone calls Mommy, would fuss over each one of us. I was always overfed. I ate until I couldn't, and she always asked me, "But Senah, why don't you *eat*? Are you well? It makes me think you are not well?" She was on the verge of tears, trying to make sure I wasn't pulling a fast one.

What I saw in everyone and everything was a kind of focus that both demanded and transcended patience. Everything required greater effort and thus greater care, greater attention; the repetition was expressed as a kind of nonchalant precision, but the impatience and convenience I had grown up with simply does not respect or allow for this level of effort. I saw my mother reflected there and even glimpsed some muted echo of myself. Recognizing this quality of resilience and quiet determination expressed through craftsmanship and modality was what first led me to reconsider the fact that my mother always had tea and bread in the house, even when we were shitty broke, while I had wondered how or why she pushed herself so hard.

Of course, in this former British colony, tea was ubiquitous. But only oddballs drank tea as "tea," as leaves steeped in water. No, any self-respecting individual took their chai—the black tea that remained a staple of the regional economy—steeped in whole milk and sweetened with raw sugar. At first my stomach lurched at so much dairy, but I realized that a lot of protein was coming to me this way, as snacks became a distant memory associated with my anxious oral fixation.

Chai was served in sixteen-ounce mugs, filled out of tall thermoses that made their rounds on silver platters, after breakfast, in some singular teatime between lunch and dinner, and after dinner, of course. It was rarely served all by its lonesome. We might have rolled and cut chapati (a fried flatbread at least inspired by the local East Indian diaspora), a light but thick-cut bread with fresh butter, or mandazi, that exquisite, golden East African donut of legend. The mandazi is certainly worth doting on here, as it had a flavor that I only now, today, recognize as cornmeal, which made all the difference. It often took a form similar to donut holes. Bakeries produced mandazi then, and now, but homemade is always best, and it seemed there was always more than enough for everyone.

Fittingly, more than enough was what I got, whether I had a seat at the table or on the couch, listening to some of my cousin's first rap lyrics. As I sat cramming my face either by electric or lantern light, my cousins were always cramming for classes, copying and recopying essential notes to pass exams that would determine whether or not they could move on to the next form, to the next institution, toward a more abundant future. I saw in their drive my mother, then tried to imagine the girl she had been, pushing just as hard, for all the same reasons. I thought about how different I was from her, how much easier things had been for me, how much lower the stakes. And then I tried to let it go.

Depending on when I woke up and what was around, lunch and dinner included more staples of the diet in the family compound. The area itself was just off Balintuma Road and consisted of grassy lawns and a smattering of one-story bungalows connected by short, winding dirt paths. There were pit latrines tucked away here and there, shower stalls for bathing, and fenced-off plots where food grew. The area was lightly landscaped so that there were places to wash clothes and recessions for the waste-water to run off; there was no indoor plumbing, no gas lines; electricity was spotty at best most days. The homes were quite small compared to anything I'd seen in the United States, but almost no one lived alone. A courtyard with a willow tree one of my uncles had planted was the place where we hosted guests, in what had been my jaajaa's house. On hot days, we took papyrus mats onto the veranda, where much of the cooking and conversation took place. May it ever be so.

There were what I called the hard starches that included green matoke, cassava, and white rice, of course, though I am not sure of the variety. But what I found to be the most fabulous and mystical of these was the lumonde. I had never eaten a potato so sweet and so white as the "Irish" potato I was accustomed to in the states. Any of these hard starches could be boiled and mashed, typically over a coal-fire sigiri, no mean feat, especially when you are feeding a hungry clan numbering up to two dozen on any given week. The matoke was particularly intriguing because its incredible starchiness made the process so involved, especially when going for volume. The sigiri ovens were a hack to get around the fact that no one on our upper-middle-class property had natural gas. The matoke had to be softened before pounding, but at the same time it was crucial to retain the moisture, so they were often soaked for hours before being pounded. The matoke were wrapped in leaves from the small palms of the plant, and the bundle was placed in a pot lined with the stems, which also accentuated the natural flavor. Only after some time would they be pounded into mush, with water added periodically to get the texture right.

Now, matoke was always a starch used to supplement a protein, which was stewed, fried, or grilled. Perhaps that might mean a groundnut sauce with what I secretly called "ultraviolet greens." These greens were never just green, always an almost wine-dark violet. They had that same bitter something as collards. We might eat them alone or in the manner described above. But they were always at least boiled tender, never served in some kind of cold salad form. The groundnut, too, was critical, although more of a recurring guest star than a core cast member.

Versatile and cheap, the groundnut goes with anything and everything. Have them shelled and oven-roasted with salt: simple. Pound them down for flour, a base for groundnut sauce, like with those greens, and it's next-level. But take that same sauce and sauté it over onion and smoked catfish or tilapia, and it's something special. Here, too, I found a kind of circular, nostalgic logos that rendered my mother and her point of view in sharper focus. Here is the one thing that, given time and care, can be cultivated and transformed to be eaten, absorbed, consumed, understood, personified in manifold textures, temperaments, flavors. But that thing remains itself, in essence, and as such unchanged. This is what my mother's mind, body, and spirit are made of, the flesh and blood born of Uganda, pearl of the African continent. This legacy was ours to inherit, absorb, embody, and uphold, so long as we live, before, after, and again, wherever we are.

I remembered my mother finding that focus beyond patience while her bratty son flitted around her, breaking action figures out of "cryogenic stasis," and understood better who she is, who I am, in a way that no words we might've shared could ever do justice. We had clashed, not physically but violently, for so long, and would continue to do so, but I could respect her struggle, her character, her elemental nature in ways that deepened my love for her, ways that gave me a history that wrapped around and through time as I had been trained to understand it. For that, I offer her my eternal gratitude.

Sitting in 2020 with my cousins, whom I met as small children and toddlers half a world away, I felt safe and secure in knowing we grow and share a history to which we are each a living monument. I was relieved to find my lifeblood replenished on every level in the fellowship of my flock, no matter how black a sheep

I may be, no matter how we are pushed to adapt and negotiate this strange new world. Now, *banange*, we are adults, beginning to have children, to find love, to venture forth into the world and challenge the low expectations of mainstream narratives with the complexity and dynamism we feed to one another and season to suit our palates. We learned from watching our parents in the kitchen. It's what we were raised on. It's what we're made of.

. . . .

Senah Yeboah-Sampong is a writer, warlock, and imagineer. His love for story has blended his interests in history, graphic literature, and Afrofuturism. His writing and reporting have appeared on KFAI and MNArtists.org and in the *Spokesman Recorder, Science, Mshale,* and *Greenroom Magazine.* Senah self-published "The Overview Effect" with Jake Olson in 2018.

Fragments of Food Memories; or, Love Letter to My Dad

· · · · · · · · · · · · · · · · ·

Lina Jamoul

Ahmad

My dad loved to cook, and I loved to eat his food. Sliced courgettes with scrambled eggs; a simplified "lazy" dish of a complicated convoluted dish called fattet bettenjan—a layered dish of the following: rice (on my urging); fried kibez/bread (his twist; you're supposed to just toast it in the oven); eggplant with ground beef in tomato sauce, covered with yoghurt/tahini sauce; roast chicken and potatoes; homous (pureed chickpeas); mtabal (pureed eggplant).

I was taller than my father even though he wouldn't admit it. Brown eyes, intense eyebrows, looked younger than his years and hard life, used to have dark hair that had grayed and thinned out, a goatee—also graying. He was aneek—put together. Wore a newsboy hat, which he pulled off because he was an intellectual (self-described); carried a leather shoulder bag—square and structured with zips and different compartments. His pipe and tobacco went in the first compartment. He took pride in his appearance. His uniform was dark gray pants with a button-down checkered shirt and burgundy or gray V-neck sweater and a tan light jacket.

My father had been politically exiled from his home country Syria since 1977. A quiet, intense, sometimes angry, yet sensitive and soulful man who took pride in not conforming to tradition.

Arab Patriarchy

Of course, in the tradition of Arab patriarchy he had more ability than most to not conform. Yes, his nonconforming, oppositional ways cost him his ability to live in and visit his home country, but his other ways of nonconforming—womanizing, drinking, speaking his mind—the Arab patriarchy could tolerate.

My father, the middle-to-old child of nine siblings, relished when others expressed their love for him; he liked attention, and he was proud of being a good cook, which is an anomaly in Arab patriarchy. His girlfriend would remark with wonder, "Ahmad does all the cooking," and he would pretend not to hear and smile smugly.

Arab patriarchy is like machismo culture. Being in the kitchen and raising children are squarely women's domains. I mean, sure, women work and go outside, but public life is still not fully and freely accessible to all of us. Patriarchy is on a spectrum: on the one end with laws like Saudi Arabia and on the other with the intrusive male gaze, which can be verbal or physical, that communicates *don't get too comfortable; this is my space.*

Two Different Dates

Four years ago, on the one-year anniversary of my father's passing, give or take a day or two, I wanted to commemorate his life and express my love for him by cooking his signature dish, makloube, which means upside down in Arabic.

I can never remember the exact date of my father's death because he passed on two different dates. When they called me, it was Tuesday in the early hours of the morning in Algeria, and in Minneapolis it was Monday in the evening. These aren't just dates; they are distance. It matters because it means I wasn't there. The eight-hour time distance represents a geographical distance, from Minneapolis to Algiers, that needed to be bridged if I was to see him one last time and witness his burial. But there was also political distance. Since the war in Syria, and the outpouring of Syrians fleeing for their safety, Syrians were not allowed to enter Algeria without a visa. And so for the first time in the twenty-some years I'd been visiting him, to enter the country I needed a visa, which takes an obscene amount of time to get. It took traveling to New York, pulling a million strings, paying a bunch of money, and eventually it was late Thursday afternoon when I got to his apartment and collapsed crying in the arms of his best friend. It took four days to bridge the eight-hour time difference. On Friday, we buried him.

Bettenjan—Eggplant—Aubergine

My dad made makloube when we were all living together, before my mum became a single mum. Back then he didn't do all the cooking—he would cook this one dish. And I hated it. Because it had eggplant, and I hated eggplant. I would push aside the eggplant and just try to eat the rice and the meat, but the eggplant slime would get all over. Makloube is served with yoghurt, and that made it more palatable.

I don't remember when I started to love it exactly. What I know is that to me as a kid eggplant was bitter and slimy. I avoided it, which is hard to do because it's so prevalent in Arab cooking—aubergine sandwiches, stuffed eggplant, pureed eggplant, fried eggplant. Maybe I started loving it when my taste buds matured, and things that tasted bitter and I disliked as a kid—eggplant, mushrooms, mloukhia—I started to like. Not just like, but love.

Mloukhia

Mloukhia—like eggplant—tasted bitter and slimy to me as a kid. It's green; its appearance is a lot like spinach. It's dried—I remember, in Syria, the mloukhia would be put on folded-out newspapers to dry overnight. We would have it with chicken or beef. And rice on the side with shereya (thin, vermicelli noodles).

I loved the rice, could tolerate the meat, and hated the slimy, bitter mloukhia.

In fact, I hated mloukhia so much that I kicked a dish out of my mother's hands when we were still in Syria. I didn't mean to. I was just kicking away, having a tantrum because I wanted to eat rice with shereya, which I loved and still love to this day. But the plate caught my foot, and the food went flying on the floor, and that was a super disrespectful thing to do because of feet and food in the Arab world. It was the only time my mother has ever smacked me. I think it was on my thigh.

I don't know when it changed, but now I love the smell, the texture, the taste. By my early twenties, mloukhia and makloube would become my favorite foods.

When you go "home," which for me includes visiting my uncle and his family in Texas, people ask what you want to eat. Shou shtaheti? *What do you yearn for?* A specific word for yearning related to food, and I would ask for mloukhia and makloube.

Whenever my mum visits me in Minneapolis from London, she makes mloukhia—and sometimes it turns out good and sometimes not so much because Arabs don't use recipes and she's not a great cook.

My Mum's Cooking

I love food. Food is comfort, joy, desire, luscious. It wasn't always this way. I used to not care for food. Maybe because my mum didn't really know how to cook. I started liking food when I learned how to cook. I'm a better cook than my mother. She tells the story of when she was married, she called her friend and asked her how she could make eggs. The middle-to-old child of a family of eight or nine—I forget. And her mother had been married off at fifteen or sixteen or eighteen. It depends who tells the story, but young. Now, my grandmother could cook. And my dad can cook. He loves to cook and loves to eat. I still write about him in the present tense even though he's been dead five years in August. My mum loves to eat and hates to cook.

It was a mark of pride as a woman to be a good cook. As I became a teenager and grew into my late teens and early twenties, relatives would ask me, *Do you know how to cook?* My mum took pride in saying she didn't like to cook—almost as much pride as my dad took in being a good cook. Maybe it was one of their many acts of rebellion. Along with my mother, who came from established and well-to-do Damascus people, a Sunni whose family is said to have lineage to the Prophet Muhammad (peace be upon him), marrying my father from a modest family, from a small rural town, an Ismaili—a Shi'ite sect considered by some as not being really Muslim. And their rebellion to participate in the workers party—a secular, left-wing group—in opposition to the Assad government and the Soviet Union that backed him.

My mum took as much pride in not knowing how to cook as she did in not wearing the hijab, marrying an infidel, reading Trotsky, going off to university, and wearing miniskirts. And she didn't teach me to cook, nor did she teach me to sew, or to put on makeup. She taught me to love to read and gave me books.

But she also knew that while books might nourish the soul, they don't—literally—nourish the body. And when she became a single mum, she made every effort to have a home-cooked meal for me. She was proud of that. Years later, sitting in my Minneapolis kitchen, she would say to me, *Do you know that I made sure you had a home-cooked meal because I knew how important nutrition was even though I hated to cook.* (She knew salad was important, but she's not a cook so she would cut up one tomato in chunks and season it with salt on the side of my home-cooked meal.) She was equally and simultaneously proud of these two different facts that seemed to contradict each other.

Family

Arabic food is amazing. I want to eat it all the time. All the time. I want to eat homous. Mostly I want to eat my dad's and my grandmother's cooking—and they're both dead. Everything else is cheap imitation. Food is so bound to family. And family is where you come from. My mum's family is from Damascus. They ate in a very refined way, in that they always had lots of options in the meal. They had stuffed courgettes and mloukhia and kebbeh.

My dad's family came from a small town. They ate borghol and eggs. My dad said that borghol is the staple food of his town. Borghol (bulgur) is a wheat grain that can be used like rice. You can have borghol with lentils, or you use it to make tabouleh. When my dad first brought my mum to his hometown, Salamieh, to meet his family, the boys catcalled, *she doesn't look like she was raised on borghol.* This story was told by my dad. I asked him what that meant, and he said it meant she obviously wasn't from there. The stories—like the recipes—are passed on by my dad and not my mum, who was too busy telling me to make sure I did my homework and made my bed.

Borghol is like rice, but more textured and with a more earthy flavor. It can also be clumped up and soft. It's very satisfying to eat, and fills you up fast. It's great with lentils; the flavors and textures complement each other. One has crunch and smoothness (lentils), while the other is soft and grainy (borghol).

I remember the eggs my grandmother—my dad's mum— would cook. They were the most delicious, and they came from the chickens in her yard. I vaguely remember the chickens. I vividly remember the eggs. Out of every taste in my childhood, I remember my grandmother's eggs the most. We'd have them for breakfast. She'd scramble them—softly scrambled eggs, salted. We'd have khibez—bread, pitta bread, except it wasn't like the pitta bread you get in the Upper Midwest. It was round, flat, and big. Instead of utensils or your individual plate, you'd have the khibez. You tear off a bite-size bit of bread and fold it in your right hand. Put the bread piece on the egg and pinch or fold to scoop up the eggs with the bread and put them both in your mouth.

We'd eat sitting on the floor in the same spot where my grandma—my siti—would sleep and I next to her. So content. The freshness of the eggs; the roughness of my grandmother's hands but the gentleness of her touch. She'd scoop me up and sniff me and say, *You smell like Ahmad* (my father, whom she hadn't seen since 1977 and would never see again—unless, of course, they're together in heaven). The eggs tasted more—more fully like eggs, more flavorful—and the texture: creamy, fluffy. What I wouldn't give to go back and have scrambled eggs and khibez with my grandmother. I always get excited to try the freshest farm eggs in Minneapolis. Currently, a friend sells us her friend's farm eggs. And they're good. But they're not the same as my grandmother's eggs.

I remember these scenes like fragments. Like a lost language. A language I once kind of knew—as much language as a seven-year-old knows. It's like stunted growth. My Arabic—food, language, culture—stopped growing at seven years old. It's as mature as a seven-year-old. And here I am, a grown-ass forty-two-year-old woman, with all the sophistication and wits of a fully fledged, developed adult, yet the things that are core, most of who I am— my identity, foundation, base—function with the maturity and development of a seven-year-old.

What does a seven-year-old like to eat? Chicken. Bread. Chocolate. Macarona. Cheese. Drink? Tea.

But it's not that simple because I went back. I developed other food memories. Like Algerian pizza, which is fucking delicious. Doesn't taste quite like any pizza I had in America, which doesn't taste quite like any pizza I had in Italy—but it's still fucking delicious. It's not only Americans who can bastardize food. But it's only Americans who can make the bastardization universal. As my dad aged and after his stroke, he had less energy. Less energy to go outside, walk, be social, cook. And so for the first time he would get takeout. Our takeout was Algerian pizza. It didn't come in different sizes, and you couldn't order slices. The dough was thin and soft. The crust was like thin New York pizza, but even thinner and softer. Tomato sauce and cheese, but less cheesy and less tomatoey; it was more subtle. Other toppings included olives and mayonnaise.

We Don't Bake

Arabs don't really bake. It's too precise, particular, and you have to pay attention to timing. There is little precision, few specific ingredients, and not a lot of attention to exact timing in Arab cooking. We throw things together—every family does it differently—and a lot of it is by instinct, smell, taste. I don't remember ever seeing a recipe or a recipe book until I was in my twenties and living in the UK—al ghourbe, the strange land.

There are so many different ways to make something.

I guess that's why you were either a good cook or you weren't. If my mother had some recipes to follow, she might have been a better cook.

Coffee and tea are as important as food. Tea you have when you eat breakfast. But all other hot beverages are consumed *after* you eat, not during the meal.

Imagine my horror when I moved to the UK and people were drinking tea with their supper—also their tea. In England, the word for "dinner" or "supper" or whatever is "tea." That's just crazy. Language is as weird and particular as food.

Makloube

Makloube became one of my favorite dishes. And the dish I would cook in memory and honor of my dad. Makloube: it's descriptive of something that's been turned upside down. Like our lives? It's called that because after the food has finished cooking in the pot, you flip the pot and all its contents upside down. You do that by first putting the tray face down—upside down—on top of the pot. Then you swing the pot with the tray in place—upside down. And then the tray becomes the right side up, with the pot—and all its contents—becoming upside down. You let it sit and take shape for a few minutes. And then after a while, you lift the pot delicately, and what should remain is the food upside down in the shape of the pot it was made in. I have no idea why you turn it upside down. It's exactly the same food contents; it tastes exactly the same; it's actually pretty hard to turn it upside down. Yet, from this totally inconsequential—taste-wise—act is derived the name of the dish. In terms of presentation, it's very consequential. In fact, the more the food content retains the shape of an upside down dish, the more successful you'll have been.

When I made it, it was my white American husband who flipped the dish upside down. Half of it retained the shape of the pot, and half of it fell apart. There was no consequence to the taste of the dish.

My father's kitchen was narrow in a small, one-bedroom apartment on the sixth floor in a building in Algiers where the elevator had stopped working at least ten years earlier, maybe more.

The narrow kitchen had French doors, probably because it had been built by the colonizing French, that opened to a small, narrow balcony where the laundry hung out to dry. In the corner, right next to the French colonizing balcony doors, was a sink: white, low, wide. At times the water would get shut off, so under the sink on the tiled floor were barrels filled with water. A plastic, round container filled with water and soap was used to wash the dishes. Opposite and on the wall were hooks where my father hung the different-sized pans. Next to the sink was the stove: white, small by American standards, normal by everywhere else standards. Next to the stove was a counter made of stone: heavy, durable, solid. He would lay out old newspapers to protect it.

He would also lay out old newspapers to cover the low table where we ate in the living room, which functioned as a dining room and office and, at night, as one of the bedrooms. The newspapers were an easy substitute for tablecloths.

On the counter was where he would prep the magic.

He would soak the rice in cold water. The lamb chunks, already cut by the butcher, he would sprinkle with salt. He would peel and slice the aubergines on the counter. He would salt the aubergines so they didn't "drink" too much oil. In his largest frying pan—where he kept oil that he would reuse; I don't know how many times—he would lay the individual slices of aubergine. He would heat the second- or thirdhand oil in the pan and submerge the aubergine slices. Deep-fried aubergine slices. Yum. Put them in pitta bread—khibez—and they make amazing sandwiches. Once the aubergine slices were browned, he would carefully remove them and set them aside on a plate. He would lay out the rest of the slices in the sizzling oil. It would take about two to three rounds for him to deep-fry all of his salted aubergine slices.

I can never bring myself to use the same amount of oil he does, which means that I flip the aubergine over once they are browned on one side. I also lay them on paper towels to remove excess oil.

Now was time for the meat. He would fry the lamb chunks in a drop of oil until they were brown all over. Then he would add some kamoon (cumin). Then he would add water and let the lamb cook.

I must confess to not remembering what he would do next. He didn't enjoy having me around in his small kitchen while he cooked. There's no place to sit, and it was barely big enough for one person to be doing their thing.

Cooking was a meditative process for my dad, so he liked to be alone for it. He tolerated me for a bit, and then I could tell he wanted me out of there. He enjoyed telling me how to do this and that, but I never wrote it down and remember only fragments.

And so when I cook his recipes, they're part memory, part Googling similar recipes, and part adaptation.

So this is how I make the makloube: Add water and spices to the browned lamb. Let it stew for about an hour or so, then remove and save the stock.

Arrange the chunks of meat in a big cooking pot; layer the eggplant on top. Add the rice and then the stock from when you boiled the meat. Cover and simmer for about twenty minutes.

Once the stock has been absorbed, the magic happens. And you flip it. Serve with yoghurt.

One-Year Anniversary

That evening in Minneapolis was the first time I'd cooked makloube in my entire life. Earlier in my life, I ate it often, and always when I visited my dad in Algeria because he would always make it. I wish my father was alive so I could ask him why that was his signature dish, where he learned to make it. I invited ten or so friends to share the meal and asked everyone to tell stories about their fathers.

I bought the lamb from Seward Co-op and ran into someone I know from my work for a labor union. Our union represents fifteen thousand state employees. She had been a member, but she left to work for Ramsey County because the pay was better and she had been sexually harassed on the job, and there's a statistic—eighty percent (maybe?)—of women or employees who are harassed at work end up leaving. When she left, she wrote to me and a few others that her work with and through the union helped her find a voice she didn't know she had. She fought to get sexual harassment processes changed in the state—and won. She fought for—and won—paid parental leave for state employees because when she had her son she realized how difficult it was not to have paid time off for the birth of her child.

I don't know if it was a coincidence or not when I ran into her at the co-op picking up organic lamb to cook for my my-father-is-dead-I-love-my-father meal. But I remember that day as I remember her. Where does it fit? It fits in who I am, who I've become, what I do, and what I contribute to the world. On occasion I'll cook my father's food and reminisce. But every day my vocation, my work, is in his honor and testament to him and his work, his belief, his sacrifices—and the sacrifices we made as a family. He fled Syria in 1977. Countless more have fled since. The calling he felt—a conviction that a better, more just world was possible—also calls out to me, and I respond. Less of a conscious decision, more of a call and response in my bones. And there's no recipe.

. . . .

Lina Jamoul was born in Damascus, Syria, and has lived in Syria, Cyprus, London, Chicago, and Minneapolis. She is a labor and community organizer by day and theater artist and writer by night. She has a PhD in geography from Queen Mary University of London.

Mov Ntse Dlej

. . . .

Kou B. Thao

Insatiable

Every Hmong child grew up eating mov ntse dlej (rice mixed with water), whether they were raised in Chiang Mai, Thailand, or Milwaukee, Wisconsin. Even I, the first Hmong person ever born in New Jersey, knew the joys of being handed a bowl of warm rice doused in cold water. Mov ntse dlej is steamed short-grain white rice mixed with water to make it easier for children to eat. Sometimes the rice is freshly cooked, and other times it's left over from the day before. This quintessential dish may seem oddly bland unless you are Hmong. Even as an adult, when I think about mov ntse dlej my mouth starts to water and my throat yearns to be quenched.

My mind drifts back to rare weekends when my mom didn't have time to cook and my dad was in charge of dinner. Most often dinners with dad were beef jerky and mov ntse dlej. At the time, my younger sister, Melinda, and I always complained and asked if we could order pizza instead. However, looking back, there was something refreshing and comforting about slurping the cold water out of the rice bowl after a salty bite of jerky.

My dad would scold us, saying we were lucky to be eating meat at all. He'd tell stories of growing up poor in the villages of Laos and how all they had to eat was rice mixed with water and hot pepper. The chunks of beef jerky accompanying our rice bowls were *luxuries*.

Stories of food were often accompanied by tales of how he had to walk through the jungle for five days past tigers to reach his elementary school. This lesson was thrust upon us whenever we didn't want to wake up for the school bus. "You are lucky you have a bus!" he'd yell.

My father's accounts of the past were weapons of guilt, but he never divulged further details of his life. Melinda and I had no reference point in our Americanized minds for these monologues, so his attempts to scold us for not appreciating how good we had it were lost on us. My father never spoke about how he, my mother, and my older sister, A, and older brother, Xue, fled Laos during the fall of Saigon and were forced into Thai refugee camps.

In reality my parents were the ones assaulted by guilt—stemming from not being able to provide food for my siblings during those difficult times. My family was one of the first Hmong families to come to the United States after the end of the Vietnam War in 1975. My father was a fifth-grade elementary school teacher in Laos; therefore, he was exempt from joining the Central Intelligence Agency's "Secret Army" of Hmong-Lao guerrilla fighters battling the Communists during the Vietnam War. My uncle was a second lieutenant for the CIA; he spoke English, Hmong, Lao, Thai, and French. His rare language skills and connections helped him, his wife and children, our family, and my father's siblings and their families to be among the first to escape to Thailand. After seven months in the Ban Vinai refugee camp,* they boarded a plane and landed in Pella, Iowa, in 1976. My father tells stories of being amazed that clouds fell from the sky in Iowa—it was his first time seeing snow. A kind Iowan family agreed to sponsor our family; thus the land of tulips became their new home.

---

*The Ban Vinai Thai refugee camp was the largest camp for Hmong fleeing Laos during the Vietnam War, holding about 45,000 refugees.

My parents' first decade in the United States was spent in poverty, working janitorial and factory jobs. By the time Melinda and I were born, they had relocated to New Jersey and clawed their way into the middle class through a combination of hard work and frugality. Being middle class came with luxuries like Christmas presents, McDonald's Happy Meals, and a bottomless refrigerator. Our older siblings teased Melinda and me for not having to worry about food stamps and for actually getting what we wanted for Christmas. When they were young, if they got presents it was usually socks. One Christmas when I was in middle school, my dad got me the Notorious B.I.G. album because it was on my wish list. (He soon regretted this gift after I blasted it on the CD player.) Not only was putting food on the table something that brought my parents pride, taking us to fast food restaurants was a way to prove that we had assimilated: we were American.

I would soon learn that "being American" had its costs. As I got older, fast food and no exercise caught up with me. When we went shopping for church clothes, I was resigned to shopping in the "husky" section for boys. I also had braces and transition lens glasses that transformed from translucent to mahogany brown in the sun. In sum, I was the walking epitome of awkward.

My parents consciously erased Hmong history, culture, and spirituality from our lives. We went to a white Christian church and attended Vacation Bible School every summer with my white Christian classmates. My dad spoke only English to us, while my mom spoke mainly Hmong, but we responded in English. "Lus noj hmo!" my mom would yell at us to come and eat dinner. "Our TV show is not done, Mom!" we'd usually whine in return. Village life in Laos or the bombs of war were the farthest things from my childhood experience—which was exactly what my parents wished for us.

My parents' other wish was for me to become a doctor—to live the American dream. Luckily, school came easily to me and

I earned As without much effort. Outside of school, my sister and I were usually home alone. My two older siblings married and moved out of the house, and my parents both worked second shift. Food and television were our babysitters.

I loved the freshly prepared dinners my mother always left on the stove. Melinda and I would come home from school, drop our backpacks on the kitchen floor, and peek under Butterfly Gold Corelle plates atop bowls of warm food. Some days there were freshly fried egg rolls; other days there was ground beef and bell peppers stir-fried in oyster sauce. The beauty of Hmong food is that it is an amalgam of the cultures of the many places Hmong have lived throughout history—China, Vietnam, Thailand, Laos, and now America. Melinda and I shrieked with joy whenever we removed the plate to reveal a baking pan filled with my mom's infamous dish—meat loaf! Somehow her meat loaf was always incredibly juicy, bursting with flavor and melting in my mouth like butter. Her secret ingredient? Lipton's onion spice packets.

My mother had an intimate knowledge of Lipton's products, having worked in the Lipton factory for nearly ten years. With a fifth-grade education in Laos, she was able to find only factory work in the states. My mom is the kindest and most hardworking person I know. She is only five feet tall—five foot three if you count her perm—but her warm and bright personality makes her seem much bigger. She shows her love through food, which was evident throughout our childhood. My mom is a master chef and a student of global cuisine. She sees something prepared once and can mimic the flavors to a T. Once while I was visiting home, she was making empanadas and chimichurri sauce from scratch. I grabbed a freshly fried empanada and took a bite. A flavor bomb exploded in my mouth, fireworks bursting from my eye sockets. It tasted like the empanadas from my favorite Argentinian steak house in Chicago, where I was living at the time. "Ma! How do you know how to make these?" My shouting was muffled by a mouthful of meat.

"My friend from work showed me," she stated casually, continuing to stuff meat into pockets of pastry dough. Another time I came home and she was making Vietnamese bánh xèo from scratch. The bright yellow crepe batter was perfectly crisp in my mouth, contrasting with the succulent, savory filling of pork, shrimp, and bean sprouts. The sweet-salty fish sauce and lime dip added a bright splash of umami that brought me back to the Viet restaurants I frequented in Chicago on Argyle Street. The dish was yet again a product of inviting her factory friends over to swap family recipes. Though my mother never traveled to any of the places where these dishes originate, she lived out her hunger for travel through food—the flavors and textures satiating her curious and adventurous spirit. The upside to having spent decades toiling away in factories was cultivating friendships with other hardworking mothers from around the world.

My mother inspired my love of cooking and food. There is a feeling of freedom that comes with cooking: experimenting with ingredients, creating concoctions that magically meld. As a kid, a favorite after-school snack was bologna and rice tacos. Melinda and I would each fold a slice of bologna like a taco, take a steaming scoop of jasmine rice out of the rice cooker, and place it into the mysterious deli meat. The clump of bland rice perfectly balanced the salty, slimy bologna. That is the magic of rice—it always takes on the flavors of whatever you eat it with. We would munch on our bologna tacos while watching our favorite after-school shows—*DuckTales* and *Saved by the Bell*.

With my parents at work, television was a faithful babysitter and taught me several life lessons as a child. It taught me that white jocks are to be desired. I learned that Asians don't exist in the media. I discovered it is bad to be fat. I learned that it is wrong for boys to be feminine or emotional. Yet here I was, a chubby Asian boy who would rather brush the hot pink mane of Melinda's My Little Pony than try to throw a football. I was not white or skinny enough to fit in at school. Where did I belong in this world? My isolation pushed me closer to my solace—food. Food was always there to comfort me and to numb my negative thoughts. But though I was fat, I was never full.

Hungry

Throughout my suburban public school education, from kindergarten to high school I was surrounded by white classmates and the occasional sprinkle of other races. I knew little about what it meant to be Asian American and even less about what it meant to be Hmong aside from my bologna tacos and our occasional jerky and mov ntse dlej dinners. I pretended I was white at school. Like the rice in my bologna tacos, I blended into my surroundings, taking on the flavors of the people around me. Blending in got more complicated as I grew older. Early on I knew I was different. Soon my racial identity was not the only thing I tried to hide.

With each passing year my attraction to other boys grew stronger. And with each passing year I pushed those yearnings down deeper. I buried them along with my questions about who and what is Hmong. Whenever I asked questions about being Hmong or about the past, my dad would begin to tear up or change the subject. I quickly learned to stop asking questions about those topics. We were American and we should be grateful. We were rebuilding a new life and I was going to be a doctor. Excelling in school was a welcome distraction to bide my time; it helped me craft my identity and sense of worth.

By middle school, puberty was beginning to run its course. I was getting taller, which was stretching out my fat and making me less rotund. Middle school made me hyperconscious about my weight and my sexual identity. In sixth grade, the SlimFast diet was all the rage, and I gladly hopped on the bandwagon. My transition glasses were replaced with blue contact lenses, and I discovered hair gel and name brand clothes. I continued to excel in school. On the outside, everything seemed to be coming together. On the inside, I was a mess.

Middle school was when I started binge eating, fasting, and yo-yo dieting. These habits continued into high school and college. I was hyper-focused on my weight and my physical appearance. I cultivated a well-manicured facade as a National Honor Society member, the editor in chief of the high school newspaper, the lead in school musicals, and an active member of my church youth group. Privately, I was having panic attacks when contemplating whether I was really gay and whether anyone would love me if they knew the truth—all the while binging on food to soothe these frenetic fears. Binge sessions would be followed by intense workouts to burn what I ate. On the outside, I never had a hair out of place (literally—I went through a lot of gel and hair spray). I was known by friends for always carrying a comb in my pocket and having a mirror in my locker. This foresight was something I learned from my dad, who always had a comb in his back pocket and Tic Tacs in his front pocket. Appearances were everything to him.

My hard work in academics led to a full scholarship to college in Philadelphia and subsequently full scholarships for two master's degrees and my doctoral studies. (My father decided a PhD would suffice in lieu of an MD.) Despite all this success, I still didn't feel I was good enough. My studies and my community work led me around the world. After Philadelphia, I lived in London, the Bay Area, Chicago, and Thailand. My mother's global cooking skills contributed to my eventual evolution into a foodie and my travels around the world in search of delectable dishes to delight my palate.

I was the first in my family to return to Southeast Asia. I spent a summer working with a nongovernmental organization (NGO) in Khek Noi, the largest Hmong village in Thailand. There were many things that surprised me that summer. One of them was the food. It was delicious, home-cooked, and fresh from the market each day. It was also communal. I lived and worked in a shelter for

Hmong street children and ate each meal with the staff and kids. Food was about nourishment, community, and caring for one another. This communal experience was a first for me; growing up, Melinda and I practically raised ourselves and mostly ate alone. This tendency extended into adulthood. Particularly in graduate school, I spent so much time studying and working that my meals were had in my few minutes to spare while reading a book or staring at my computer. But in the village, food was special, meat was prized, and communal meals were valued. The NGO was able to provide for the children, so we had meat at almost every meal—a rarity for most of the impoverished villagers.

Hmong meals are served in threes (not counting the rice)— soup, a side dish, and an entrée. I loved sitting down at the table to discover what delicious Hmong-Thai concoctions my colleagues had cooked up: squash curry, ground pork stir-fried with basil and chili peppers, boiled chicken soup and greens, omelets, sizzling eggplant, and more. Some of my fondest memories in Thailand were sharing meals with my kids and laughing together. I was beginning to understand that food could be healing. I will never forget those cherished moments.

In addition to filling my stomach, my time in Thailand helped fill a gaping hole in my heart: I finally learned what it meant to be Hmong. In my time there, I retraced the wounds that the war had left behind. I stumbled upon distant relatives who had not seen my parents since they were separated while fleeing Laos. I met refugees who were in hiding; we cried together as they begged me not to forget that they were still there suffering. For them, seeing me—a Hmong American—represented hope, something they had not felt in a long time. I met mothers who were so emaciated they could not breastfeed their babies or afford formula. My soul wept with each of them as our lives became entwined in those intimate moments. The depths of poverty I witnessed were gut-wrenching and branded into my brain with a searing-hot iron rod of reality. These are encounters the heart does not forget. I finally understood what my father was trying to tell me in those fleeting stories of all he had endured as a child. Those stories were not weapons of guilt; they were lessons I did not know how to learn.

In Thailand, I was also blessed to witness profound kindness and joy. I was invited to eat with Hmong elders who had just met me. I spoke with Hmong vendors at the night market in Chiang Mai and, upon mentioning I had not been to their village yet, was invited to travel with them two hours up the mountain and to stay at their home. Such radical hospitality is a pillar of our community. Wherever you go in the world, if you meet another Hmong person they will invite you to have a meal at their home and offer you a place to rest your head. Though we have been fractured by war, the ties that bind us are an inherent willingness to house and feed one another. Even if we do not know each other, we are not strangers—just estranged by global politics.

In many ways, my time in Thailand nourished a part of me that had been starved all my life: my Hmong identity. This was the part of me my parents ignored in order for us to assimilate. They thought this denial would alleviate my struggle in America. They thought erasing their past would free me from the shackles of their pain and loss. But instead the exact opposite occurred; their silence comforted them like a blanket, but when passed down it suffocated me. All my life, the mystery of our past haunted me like the ghosts of fallen Hmong soldiers in the jungles. On this trip, I was finally able to confront the apparitions, only to find that they were not lost souls to fear. Rather, they were my ancestors mourning and anticipating my return. Gay or not—they had been waiting for me to wake up and remember that I come from a lineage of warriors who relied on Mother Earth to meet all their needs.

From harvesting vegetables to raising animals to mastering herbal medicine, our deep connection to the earth kept us healthy and alive for generations. These ties were repeatedly ruptured through centuries of war and forced migration. I think about my mother and grandmother, both herbalists. When I got nosebleeds as a kid, I would yell for my mom. While other mothers might go into the bathroom for tissues, my mother would dart out the back door. She would return with a handful of leaves from her garden, instructing me to shove them up my nose. Then there were the days I would feign a stomachache to avoid going to school. Within minutes there would be a mug full of wood boiled in water, the odor filling my nostrils with a wicked stench. A tiny sip would always send me running to the bus stop. I don't know anyone in my generation who understands herbs the way my mother and grandmother do. With each generation, we are becoming more and more disconnected from the land and from the ways our ancestors have healed for centuries.

Through my time in Thailand, I began to understand what it means to truly be satiated: to be full, to be whole. I spent many of my formative years hungry to understand who I was. As my self-identity became clearer, I was pulling together pieces of myself I had buried for decades. I realized I had not become who I am in spite of being Hmong and gay. I had become who I am *because* I am Hmong and gay and so much more. It was time to reclaim these parts of myself and become whole again.

Full

In 2012 I moved from Chicago to St. Paul, Minnesota. It was my first time living in a large Hmong community, and I was *immersed*. I was working for a Hmong nonprofit organization and living in the heart of the community—a few blocks from Lake Phalen and a short drive to Hmong Village. One of the things that excited me about living in St. Paul was being able to easily access Hmong food. Hmong sausage, stuffed chicken wings, sweet pork and eggs, crispy pork belly, steamed buns, spicy papaya salad . . . I was in Hmong food heaven! (Even if I can take only two peppers in my papaya salad—I know, I'm weak.)

In Minnesota I also found the greatest sense of community I have ever felt. Because there are nearly a hundred thousand Hmong here, there is rich diversity within the community. I found my queer Hmong family here that continues to uplift me. Yet even having built a support network, I struggled with loneliness, having not found a life partner. I fell into a vicious cycle: To avoid loneliness, I threw myself into my work. But because I worked around the clock, I didn't have time to seek out relationships. In my mind, being a workaholic meant I was needed; I was worthy. Since I didn't have time to be in a relationship with an individual, I returned to the relationship most familiar to me—my relationship with food.

Food became my everything—my stress reliever, my comfort, and my confidante. And Minnesota winters, eight months of the year below freezing, made me want to inhale comfort food, pack on the pounds, and hibernate until May—allowing the fat stores to keep me warm. I gained more than forty pounds over the next few years, until the scale reached a number I had never seen above my toes—205. My BMI score danced around my plump five-foot-seven frame, taunting me like a fat-shaming tooth fairy.

After that, I decided to take control of my health. High blood pressure and high cholesterol run in my family. Both my parents have it; my puj (paternal grandmother) died of a heart attack. I made a conscious decision that that would not be my fate. I trained for a mini-triathlon, which I did two years in a row. The following year I completed a twenty-five-mile bike ride for the American Diabetes Association. I was feeling stronger and healthier, but my blood pressure and cholesterol were still high.

I realized I was not alone in facing these health issues. I have so many Hmong friends who also struggle with health concerns. In the sauna at the east side YMCA, I often overheard Hmong elders complaining about their ntshav qab zib (diabetes) and ko taw vwm (gout). Every Hmong person I know has an uncle or auntie with diabetes or gout or has it themselves. After living in

America for over four decades, the Hmong community is experiencing soaring rates of diabetes, heart disease, gout, and many other chronic conditions.

Compounding the issue is that advice from Western medical practitioners tends to contradict our Hmong diet and culture. For example, a Hmong friend of mine shared that she went in for a physical and her white doctor told her to stop eating rice. "How the hell am I supposed to stop eating rice?!" she exclaimed, flabbergasted. I think about the number of times I have heard that same medical advice. Similarly, Western doctors advise gout sufferers to not eat rich foods like beef, seafood, or pork. I understand the validity of this guidance, but these well-intentioned suggestions are offered within a vacuum that separates us as Hmong people from our histories, our families' traumatic journeys to the United States, and the sacrifices our parents have made to put food into the mouths of their beloved children. The seemingly innocuous recommendations for what we should and should not eat negate the trials our families have endured to provide rice and meat for us.

Rice has played a critical role, central to who we are and our existence. Rice is one of the few threads woven through the story cloth of our lineage, even as history books continue to erase us from global memory. When we have had nothing to feed ourselves or our children, at least we had mov ntse dlej. Saying *Don't eat rice* and *Don't eat so much meat* is a slap in the face to Hmong families who have fought for survival from the jungles of Laos to the streets of America, only to face racism, xenophobia, and hate crimes, to Hmong mothers and fathers toiling in factories and fields, underpaid and taken advantage of. It is a slap in the face to my mother; her hours spent standing in assembly lines turned to decades, eventually tearing apart her shoulder and decimating her knees, forcing her to have shoulder surgery and her right knee replaced. These are the sacrifices our families have made to put rice and meat on our tables, to fatten us up, to ensure we would never starve again.

Food is how Hmong parents show love. Most of us go a lifetime without our parents or elders ever telling us they love us verbally. But every single day, whether we are upset or have just gotten into a fight, they will still ask us, "Kov puas tau noj mov?" (Did you eat yet?). Even after criticizing how much weight we've gained, they will force us to eat more. Recently my mom turned to me in the kitchen and said, "You are so handsome." I stood still as a deer, ears perked, waiting for what I knew was sure to be a punch line. She continued, "If you just lose twenty pounds you will be even *more* handsome!" There was the arrow to the heart. She then ordered me to eat the sugar-coated donuts she had just pulled out of the fryer. This is how Hmong people show love: radical hospitality through food, through hosting, and through building community.

I'm not saying medical professionals should stop giving us advice. Rather, they need to get to know us. Learn our history; experience our radical hospitality. Move beyond the Western medical frame and integrate holistic health and wellness. Then together let's address the serious chronic illnesses that are plaguing our communities through strategies grounded in our inherent resilience. Don't punish us for surviving and blame our ailments on us. We are warriors and cultivators of the soil who have been systematically forced off our land and murdered for generations. We don't need advice given in a vacuum. We need ways to be reconnected to all that has been lost. To heal chronic illness we must first heal the wounds that have ruptured our connections to our ancestors and to the land that has always provided for us. Only then can we truly be nourished.

What are the things that we as Hmong hunger for? They are the very same things I have hungered for all my life: to be worthy, to be known, to be loved. These voids I could never fill with food, but good god did I try. I spent so much of my life not knowing who I am, denying who I am, or searching for who I am. Food was the one constant that helped me feel full in the moment. But I was never satiated. I had been using food all wrong. Food soothed my pain and anxiety, but it never addressed the root causes. I go back to the lessons I learned with my kids in the village in Thailand: when food is prepared fresh, eaten mindfully, and used as nourishment, food builds community and food heals. When we consume food from places of fear or unresolved trauma, it only temporarily covers the wounds.

I learned a Buddhist practice of mindful eating from monks at one of Thich Nhat Hanh's monasteries. Before eating, give gratitude to the land from which this food came and to the hands that harvested and prepared the food. As you chew, pay attention to the taste in your mouth; feel it swirl around your tongue. Be present to the thoughts or emotions that arise. Savor the flavors as you swallow.

When I mindfully consume a bowl of mov ntse dlej, I understand the mysteries of the mystical combination of water quenching my thirst and rice nourishing my belly. The water cleanses my palate; it washes away painful memories, like my father's fear of tigers on his way to school or bullets whizzing by his head in the dark as he carries my brother on his back across the Mekong River. The rice tastes like home; it evokes memories of my mother spoon-feeding me as a child, reminding me that I am worthy of love. The smell of steam streaming from the rice cooker brings flashbacks of my mother preparing meals in the kitchen. I remember that food, when eaten mindfully, can heal the wounds we had forgotten were there.

In trying to forget the painful memories of war, we as Hmong people forgot how it was when our hands produced everything we ate. We also forgot what makes us resilient: our Hmong identity and culture. We have had to hustle so hard to survive that we never had a chance to mourn the losses we have endured or the people we left behind. We have not had the time to acknowledge the wounds in our souls as the soles of our feet traversed continents, searching for a home that would not reject us.* We have not had time to honor the lives we have built and the feats we have accomplished here in America. We have been separated from our ancestral ways of being and knowing. Until we mourn, until we acknowledge, until we honor, we will never be able to reconnect with our ancestors and with the land.

We must reclaim the role of food in our lives—not only to relieve emaciation but also as a tool for liberation. Imagine food that not only fills our stomachs but also heals our hearts. Envision a meal where every dish honors our ancestors and every bite savors the communities we have rebuilt around us. As we approach nearly fifty years in America, we have an opportunity to dare to imagine how we will mourn, acknowledge, and honor in order to bring healing to our souls' wounds. I believe we can be the ones—our ancestors are begging us to be the ones—to transform cycles of trauma into practices of healing and resilience. Only then will our spirits be satiated, our hearts whole, and our bellies full.

. . . .

Kou B. Thao is a queer, Hmong American healer based in the Twin Cities. He is founder and CEO of LIT Consulting—Lead. Inspire. Transform. Kou holds graduate degrees from St. Joseph's University and the University of Chicago and is a 2013 Bush Fellow and a 2014 White House Champion of Change.

---

*Eduardo Duran, in his book *Healing the Soul Wound: Counseling with American Indians and Other Native Peoples* (New York: Teachers College Press, 2006), describes the soul wound as a spiritual and psychosocial rift that occurs as a result of generations of historical trauma, genocide, or forced migration.

Beans or Bullets:
A Feminist Reading of Baleadas

· · · · · · · · · · · · · · · ·

Roy G. Guzmán

> ... meaning somewhere between theorizing
> and imagining ...
>
> —Omise'eke Natasha Tinsley

The arrangement of ingredients inside baleadas may vary: beans, cheese, crème fraîche, eggs, avocados, chicken, carne asada, pork, chorizo. Preparing the dish is outrageously simple, requiring a few ingredients and an urgency to consume more than one baleada.

Baleadas are served at any time of day. Known for their quick preparation (between three and five minutes) and portability, baleadas have long been workplace staples. In the United States, flour tortillas to make baleadas can be purchased in the supermarket; in Honduras as well. But it would be an insult to the spirit of tortilla making if you relied on premade tortillas. A tortilla is not to be refrigerated. A tortilla is not to be wrapped in a damp sheet of paper towel and microwaved, although resettlement might have taught you otherwise. A tortilla is not to be treated as an afterthought but as the epicenter of a new world reverberating.

If anything, a tortilla marks life's ephemeral nature, zooming in on a bracket of time in which the circular miracle is hot. Steam rises from within as if the earth were haunted, whispering

gorgeous secrets without a care for who listens. A tortilla derives
its power from the stubborn moment. It has witnessed what days
look like without its presence. Nature is thrown into chaos for
making such sloppy mistakes.

(From a cousin's WhatsApp message) *The truth is I've made
baleadas only twice. The first time I made them they ended up
too hard. I don't know if I added enough oil or didn't let the masa
sit long enough. The second time, however, I watched a video that
mentioned all the ingredients, flour, that you need to add a bit of
salt and oil, all depending on how much masa you want to make.
You don't use too much water. I made the masa, left it alone for
about an hour, and then I made the tortilla on aluminum foil so
it wouldn't shrink. I set the comal on the stove, and this time the
baleadas came out really good. Soft. I stuffed them with refried
beans, eggs, mantequilla, and shredded cheese. They came out
so, so good! I haven't made them since. Generally, we buy them
elsewhere.*

In the myth, La Sucia's beauty and obedience are remarkable.
Honeybees for eyes or fish orbiting in small typhoons. She is
young, a quinceañera. Words from her mouth are proficient in
siestas. Her body like a saguaro's brave new arms unfolding. If
your ancestors' mouths have been hammered shut, you devise
ways to communicate with them in the language of miscompre-
hension. Intimacy, in spite of the master's rules.

Before she becomes La Sucia, she is just another brown-
skinned promise. Washes her family's clothes in a river. Knows
the women's work of devotion.

A man from a reputable family asks for her hand in marriage.
She is *to be* lucky (the infinitive form can sometimes be erased
from a sentence and the sentence remains grammatically correct). The day of their wedding, as happens in myths, plans take

a frantic turn. Because the girl is unbaptized, the priest refuses to perform any of the wedding rites. Her heartbeats feel like men going off to war. She dives into the darkest corners of depression, seizing her beauty with her. Although beauty obscured is still beauty, if it isn't objectified it can't be an object, it can't be a subject where I come from.

The could-have-been husband, put off by her condition, walks away. Forgets her. If you stare long into a white light, what was once a rumor may cease to be a rumor. Festooned in grief, the girl refuses to take off her wedding dress. To church, to the dining room, to her bedroom the dirty dress goes.

Days pass and her skin grows darker. Her eyes twist into jungles. A perfect storm transformation. One day she's told of her former lover's whereabouts. He has made a marriage proposal to another girl. The temples in her mind crumble. Owls cannot live in this darkness. She wails, as if possessed by an evil spirit. Primal tocsin.

She jumps from a cliff toward her death.

Recently, one of my husband's friends from the northern coast founded his own baleada company. But these baleadas are different. You make them with coconut milk. I tried them and they're delicious, soft, not like the ones you buy at the supermarket. Those aren't good. They're made to be sold in large quantities. But my husband's friend sells them in sets of five.

Too much history has passed through beans. So much history, in fact, that the beans are too dizzy remembering where they come from. Like people formerly colonized or settler colonial subjects.

As a child, I used to help my elders clean the beans they'd purchased in el mercado. From plastic bags to pailas, the beans would pass between our fingers on the table. We separated the good ones from the cracked ones, the good ones from the tiny rocks, from branches and leaves, from other residuals that linger after beans are gathered. Cracked beans probably faced the mouths of bugs or rodents. To a hungry belly, they are still enticing.

It may surprise an inexperienced tongue to know that Honduras makes its own distinct cheeses. There's queso seco, semiseco, fresco, fundido, quesillo. There's queso suave, fuerte, crema. There's queso frijolero, con chile, requesón, cuajada, the latter of which is usually wrapped and prepared with plantain leaves. In the same vein, crème fraîche—or what Hondurans call mantequilla rala—is not exactly crema. It's far from sour cream. It has a cool and smooth texture, is saltier than Mexican and Salvadoran cremas, is sold in plastic bags. You perforate a corner of the bag and squeeze the alabaster marvel upon the eager refried beans, the shredded cheese, between the slices of avocados, if that's how you like to rebel. Meat eaters have the option to add small pieces of fried chicken, pork, or carne asada. Grilling carne asada is a noteworthy rite among Latinxs. Variations of this meal can be found at birthday parties, picnics, Independence Day celebrations every September 15, and beyond. You spot baleadas among large festivities, awakening the taste buds in everyone's mouth.

That's what's in now, to make baleadas with coconut milk. Nowadays, when you buy them, you can choose whether or not you want them made with coconut milk. They're just delicious.

In his poem "A Valediction: Forbidding Mourning," John Donne devises the metaphor of the compass to illustrate how two lovers can be physically apart yet still tied together by their souls:

If they be two, they are two so
    As stiff twin compasses are two;
Thy soul, the fixed foot, makes no show
    To move, but doth, if the other do.

· · · · · · · · ·

These lovers are inseparable. No matter where one roams, the other is still connected. One grounds the other. I came across this image for the first time in high school. I learned it as the embodiment of faithful love between man and woman. The queer teenager in me was not welcome.

More than a decade later, I can't help seeing how Donne's lines represent more than heterosexual love. If twisted right, they can also exude nostalgia, loss, and hope.

For members of diasporic communities, the compass symbolizes the adoration they have for dishes that "just don't taste the same" outside of their vanished homelands. Yes, the baleada may be re-created in the United States, but it lacks the aura of baleadas cooked in Honduras. For example, the pair of hands that prepares the baleada en nuestra tierra mixes flour with legitimate Honduran water. The flies that briefly sit on a woman's strand of hair as she flattens the tortilla are less sophisticated than the ones in the United States, but they are nonetheless recognizable. Appetite is the needle on the compass. So are scent, taste, and texture. The baleada can exist in multiple places at once, but there is only one true baleada: the one in front of you, begging to be eaten, in the land where all of us have yet to be displaced. In the infinitive.

I love baleadas. The more simple, the better. I don't like them loaded. I prefer them with refried beans, shredded cheese, mantequilla, and that's enough. Having them with eggs and meat is just too much for my stomach.

> Prepara la mesa para diez ¡baleadas!
> Aunque vinieran solo tres ¡baleadas!
> —Banda Ibanez de Honduras, "Las Baleadas"

I was in first grade when I was asked to dance punta in front of a large crowd of parents and children at school. Punta is one of

Honduras's traditional dances whose music was put together by Garifuna people, taking from African and Arawak features. The top of my costume was yellow with black polka dots, and my dance partner was my neighbor's mulatta daughter. She was probably the first girl I fell in love with and also my first romantic disappointment when I was cautioned to not date Black girls. Mind you, my cousins' mother is Black, but somehow that didn't register when I was handed such unsolicited warning.

Upset, I made a bold move: I looked for my grandfather and asked if it was true, that I'd be disowned if I fell in love with a Black girl. He laughed, his mouth still holding on to several of his teeth. *Are you kidding?* he replied. *I never had a problem with your uncle having four kids with a Black woman. What makes you or anyone else think I care about such things?* I learned then that my family was not always open or candid with one another, even though I was told that other families, unlike ours, fought over simple things like money, parental rights, or what a person's will would state after they died.

The day of my punta performance, I gave it my all. I wanted everyone to know I was proud to dance punta and even prouder to dance it with someone I had feelings for. The crowd erupted into applause as soon as we finished dancing to "Sopa de Caracol." What I thought would make me a strong suitor in the eyes of the girl next to me turned out quite the opposite. I had outdanced her. I had become everyone's choice for lead dancer the following year. I had unintentionally outshined the girl I could see myself playing outdoors with for hours. Too much unspoken tension prevented us from ever talking like friends again.

I have tried baleadas from Trujillo, from a woman who sold them at a park. She used to prep her table and gas stove and she would make them that way. Another delicious set of tortillas for those baleadas. And like I said, they were not stuffed.

· · · · · · · · ·

Next to a baleada you might discover another blessing: el encurtido. My tolerance for spicy foods has greatly depreciated over time, but if I see an encurtido nearby, I start to drool.

Growing up in Honduras, I mostly craved chile: on tomatoes, green mangoes, rice, or scrambled eggs. The encurtido was a perfect way to capture what chile could do.

My grandmother, with whom I had a turbulent relationship until I moved to the United States and didn't see her again, somehow gave in to my cravings and prepared all sorts of spicy snacks. Some days when she would come visit us (by then she had already been living with another man for several years after leaving my grandfather), my cousins and I would compete at who would eat the most chile. Cumin, I found out, is one of chile's best allies. My grandmother would serve us slices of green mangoes and tomatoes, and we would cover them in salt, cumin, chile, and vinegar. I was always surprised that she entertained our childish antics. Perhaps, I once thought, she could see the queerness in me, so if I demonstrated how much chile I could consume, there was hope, in her eyes, that I wouldn't grow up to be such a sissy, such a disappointment to the family. From all the memories I keep of her, where I can recognize a glint of pride in her eyes, the ones about my chile-eating victories over my cousins still linger.

If chile can be added to just about anything to lend the dish an authentic Honduran flavor, baleadas are no exception. Spiciness takes many forms when supplemented to baleadas. Encurtidos, which more or less incorporate spicy pickled vegetables, are a common accompaniment. Encurtidos can be made with just a single vegetable, such as onions, and they can come off red or yellow depending on whether you add beets or other food colorings. The way I enjoy encurtidos entails slicing red or white onions, carrots, jalapeños, serrano peppers, cauliflower, beets, or radishes. Oregano, salt, spices, vinegar, garlic, sugar, and water are boiled together and then poured and mixed inside the jar with the cut vegetables. You let the encurtido perform its gentle magic for days. Chisme is had near the jar while other meals are consumed. Every so often, you check the state of the encurtido like a birth about to transpire. When it's time to welcome its blessings, you let one of the elders try it first before others are allowed. You pass the jar around, and everyone serves themselves.

I learned to make my first encurtido during home ec in elementary school. My mother and my aunt, who also raised me, helped me buy the list of ingredients the night before. In home ec, I learned to make encurtidos, repair and sew clothes, and work with wood. I assume this is what Boy Scouts learn while they're training. In Honduras, however, a lot of what is covered in vocational training is taught at home, by taking apprenticeships, or at work—sink or swim. I was very proud of my first encurtido; I don't recall making many in my lifetime, but the ones I have made have reminded me of what it's like working with my hands and producing flavors that have passed down through generations.

One of my most recent memories trying out an encurtido with a baleada took place at a Honduran restaurant in Miami. I've had the privilege to try at least three Honduran restaurants in Miami. The quality isn't always consistent. In one, the flavors are perfect, but you get small portions for a high price. In another, the dishes are cheap, but you wonder what reeks before you go in or why the restroom looks like it's never been scrubbed. Both places do take pride in how they make their own baleadas. American consumers of dishes prepared with tortillas probably can't understand how seemingly simple dishes can be botched. For those of us who grew up with tortillas, beans, or even rice, the experience can be sabotaged if something is overcooked or undercooked for a minute. A minute! Such is the love and respect we hold for the food we consume that every detail matters because our simple ways of life have mattered. Our survival, in Honduras as well as in the condition of diaspora, has always depended on how well we nurse what we put in our bodies.

. . . .

I've also tried baleadas in Utila, one of the islands, and it was the same. Another lady drew her table and gas stove, and she brought her paila with the masa balls, and she just started making them. The best thing about Utila's baleadas is that the woman would sell them along with encurtido made with onions, and that whole combination just made everything terribly delicious.

Despite there being more than 940,000 Hondurans living in the United States, only as recently as 2018 was the National Day of Baleadas declared, to be celebrated on the third Saturday of June.

Honduran historian Suyapa Portillo claims that the origin of baleadas is tied to US military interventions and the arrival of banana companies, such as United Fruit Company, to the region. They brought wheat to the north coast of the country around 1912. Another historian, Julio Cesar Zepeda, corroborates Portillo's claims, adding that many of the cooks these companies brought with them came from India and Pakistan. That is where one might find a link among the flour tortillas made for baleadas, chapati, and naan. Baleadas are, therefore, comestibles of translation.

Given its name, *baleada*—literally, a feminine-gendered person or thing that has been gunned down—the history of the baleada is murky and unruly. For instance, one claim offers the image of a person biting into the baleada, causing the pressure within to burst through the sides. Thus the beans behaved tantamount to bullets. Another claim introduces us to a woman from La Ceiba who was abandoned by her husband and decided to take out a loan to start a tortilla business to raise her five children. A tale like this demands that a woman be abandoned so that her agency can be activated. That's what machismo wants us to believe. Still, Doña Teresa, as the young woman was known, established her business near train tracks where employees of the banana companies Portillo and Zepeda tell us about commuted back and forth to work. Eventually one of these employees made a comment that the beans symbolized bullets, the cheese gunpowder, and the tortilla itself a gun. In both of these urban legends a dish is understood and mythologized through the framework of a gun. Simply put, what you eat echoes what can kill.

Yet a third famous tale epitomizes the stark reality for many women in Honduras, through what the gun itself can do. In San Pedro Sula, there lived a renowned cook who sold rolled-up tortillas. Some say she was shot to death. Others maintain that she healed from the gunshot wounds and went back to selling tortillas. When people said they were going to la baleada to buy tortillas, they meant they were going to the woman who was gunned down. At the heart of all three tales is the indisputable labor performed by women; beyond that, however, lies the menace and actual violence carried out against Honduran women. Women's labor can be understood only through a device capable of violence, or their work puts them directly in harm's way.

The fresher the tortilla, the warmer it is, the better. As soon as they are picked from the comal you eat them right away.

The spirit of La Sucia can't catch a break. La Sucia searches for her former lover among rivers and streams. In her wedding dress, the girl has set her efforts on seducing scoundrels, drunks, men who've lost their way, perhaps to gain revenge, perhaps to encounter the man who left her and finally find closure. She bewitches them in her dazzling form or in the semblance of the young bride who never got to marry.

In other countries, such as Mexico, Nicaragua, and Panama, La Sucia goes by the name La Cegua, La Siguanaba, and La Empollerada. In the urban tales that follow La Cegua, she comes out at night, cursed because of her lewdness. There are multiple Ceguas, each with their prime mission to get revenge on men, sometimes collaborating with each other to this end. They laugh and cry maniacally. Their hair often covers their face so that the prey, after staring into their eyes, can lose their minds.

One of La Cegua's stories has roots in mestizx gullibility and betrayal. La Cegua's hair is black and long like a horse's mane. Some even describe her as donning the head of a horse. She is tricked by her lover. In fact, in some of these stories, the perpetrators escape the curses that eventually befall the women, who lose their decency, status, and sanity, because the men are white and Spanish. Indigenous and mestiza women, once cursed, are unable to cross the threshold toward redemption.

The Nicaraguan version of La Sucia finds her just as ghastly, a figure cut from the same imagination from which we obtain Medusa. Only when she morphs her monstrosity into beguiling beauty is La Cegua, just like La Sucia, able to exact retribution. For men, recovery is never an option. It is typical to find in the histories that accompany these legends a man giving in to a woman's advances and thereby giving up his power. In the quest toward manhood, it is therefore necessary for a man to kill La Cegua. Only then can a man be free from women's temptation and focus on his larger, gender-based calling.

Other famous baleadas are the ones from San Pedro Sula, from a place called La Linea, because they're right by the train tracks. The train no longer runs there, but the name has stayed. Same thing there: a woman runs her business selling tortillas and baleadas. They're hot and soft.

Within a river, the part we call a pool is the deepest and slowest.

Living in Minneapolis, in the land of the Dakota and Ojibwe peoples, I have learned that water is life, that water is sacred. There may be a verb that enables us to understand this relationship at the sentence level, but contained within the element of water is the notion of life itself, the space for the sacredness. Water, in other words, *is.*

Similarly, when I speak of a pool of blood, I am bringing attention to the source that gives humans and other living things their life source, their condition for being. So then, if I write, *La encontraron baleada en un charco de sangre*, I am not just suggesting that a woman was found gunned down, drenched in a pool of her own blood. I am also suggesting that there, on the ground, is a woman who must be named. I am suggesting that a violent act was committed and that a woman's life was abruptly ended. This act typically befalls Honduran women. Scholars name this pattern femicide.

People from the coast love baleadas. They enjoy eating them in the morning, in the afternoon, and in the evening.

> I know you've got a little life in you yet
> I know you've got a lot of strength left
> I know you've got a little life in you yet
> I know you've got a lot of strength left
> —Kate Bush, "This Woman's Work"

A woman was gunned down (baleada) by eight men as she prepared to start her evening shift selling baleadas, just a few blocks away from her house. Her name was Sarin Anabel Reyes Duarte, and she was murdered without hesitation, next to her daughter.

A woman was baleada baleada baleada baleada baleada baleada baleada baleada baleada. No, this previous sentence is not a mistake but an investigation into what happens to syntax when prevalent violence and impunity fracture how victims and their communities attempt to pick themselves up afterward. In the time it took you to read that sentence, without assuming you understood what the repetitive predicate required of you, Sarin Anabel Reyes Duarte was already dead, her killers probably gone for good.

The systemic abuse Honduran women face as they try to make ends meet, as they try to visit friends and family, as they try to protect one another, is rampant. By virtue of the government's negligence, this calamity continues to propagate. Gender-motivated killings have become an ordinary phenomenon in the country. In order to avoid being baleadas, these women often run from their households and risk the dangerous journey toward the US–Mexico border. At the border, many of these women are refused due process or asylum. The Mexican and US governments collude with the Honduran government by precipitating a multinational assault on these women who have nowhere else to turn for safety. How many of these women, I wonder, got up in the morning to prepare the masa for the tortillas that would feed their partners and children? With those same hands, how many of these women have had to dig their fingers into the ground in the hopes their murdered partners and children would return? The cry of Honduran women is a cry for justice. It is a cry to have the necessary ingredients to make baleadas again, to pump the pool of blood back into the living body, so she can dream another morning into being.

Us capitalinos enjoy tortillas very much, baleadas especially, but we don't get to make them all the time.

What else is left for a woman who has been made monstrous against her will? Perhaps this unfair monstrosity is what the spirit of La Sucia seeks to redress.

Flour can be turned into many things. People nowadays make tacos with the masa. They put chicken in them, whatever they desire. As for me, I go back to the simplest way one can prepare a baleada.

. . . .

Roy G. Guzmán is the author of *Catrachos* (Graywolf Press, 2020) and the chapbook *Restored Mural for Orlando* (Queerodactyl Press, 2016). A 2019 National Endowment for the Arts fellow, they are an adjunct instructor and a PhD candidate in cultural studies and comparative literature at the University of Minnesota–Twin Cities.

The Summer of Lao Beef Jerky at Rivoli

....

Saymoukda Duangphouxay Vongsay

Mom had always wanted a porch swing for the backyard patio. For a couple of days at the start of July, Akiem and I scoured the patio furniture sections of St. Paul's hardware stores and their online offerings. We found the perfect porch swing: a deep red/white/black-striped three-seater with matching canopy on sale for $319. It looked like a dirty candy cane. It also looked comfortable. We needed that one. It was special because it was displayed on the highest shelf in the Scaffolding Tower of Deals.

The urgency was real, so we bought it immediately.

When we brought it home, everyone was ready to help assemble the porch swing, but really, it took me and my aunt Rachel (married to my father's younger brother) to assemble it correctly. Before us, the men tried and did not succeed.

In between putting all of the porch swing's accoutrements together, we snacked on rambutans. A rambutan, named after its tree, is a delicious, small, spiky red tropical fruit native to Southeast Asia. When we were growing up, rambutans cost nearly twelve dollars a pound, and it was a luxury to each have three or four fruits after dinner. It was somehow more cost-effective for the whole family to drive to Ontario for a weeklong summer visit with Uncle Shrimp than it was for us to buy a pound of rambutans from the Filipino grocery store on University Avenue. That was the late eighties and nineties. Thanks to a Hmong entrepreneur and her Mack truck that makes round trips from Florida, we now buy three or four fifteen-pound boxes of rambutans every two weeks. Twenty-three dollars a box is a small luxury.

We became pros at eating them. We pierced the deep red, spiky skins with our thumbnails, then pulled away half the shell. We didn't bother to save anything for the compost or for planting; this isn't Laos. The cracked fruit reminded me of the palace banquet scene from 1984's *Indiana Jones and the Temple of Doom*—the one where guests were served decapitated monkey heads on jewel-adorned goblets. The camera pans along the length of the banquet table as one goblet of monkey head after the other is plunked down in front of dinner guests. The camera stops and we see Indiana Jones's companion, dressed in a sari with a tikka crowning her blonde head, a goblet in front of her. The servant lifts the lid of the monkey's skull, revealing (what as a kid I imagined to be) silky, fleshy brains. She faints. The scene for me ends there. But I always think about the dessert course in that banquet hall when I'm rotating a rambutan and biting off flesh from the seed.

This is what summers taste like today and forever, I told myself.

Today until always.

After we had completed the assembly, we recruited the little ones to wipe down the sticky handles, poles, and base. No one sat on the swing to test its swingy-ness. Instead, we cleaned up. Rachel collected the plastic coverings, and I broke down the box it came in. We delegated one of the uncles to take it all away. We went back to our rambutans.

Days passed after Mom's dream porch swing was erected. It stood frozen, unused, preserved almost, on the cement patio all those days without her having sat on it. When she did the first time, she insisted on blankets. She was cold all the time now. That afternoon, we shared a bowl of lightly salted pistachios. I'm neutral about pistachios, but I would eat them with Mom so she wouldn't feel alone. Sometimes I'd take her hand into mine, place a shell on each of her fingernails, and say, *How do you like your manicure? That'll be four million dollars.* She'd laugh. She'd laugh as if that was the first time I made that joke. It certainly wasn't the first, but soon it would be one of the last.

Her hands were still strong enough to crack the shells apart then. I knew I wasn't going to hear her softly snapping pistachio shells again, and the thought brought me into a complete dejection. Throughout our days together I found myself mourning the small, soft, quiet parts of my mom: clipping fingernails over bedroom wastebaskets, pushing down the switch on the electric kettle, stirring instant Vietnamese coffee in a Corelle cup, rubbing Tiger Balm over her temples, rhythmically patting her grandbaby's thigh to lull him to sleep, peeling sour green mangos with a paring knife (the Asian way—with the knife's blade facing outward).

At the start of autumn she lost strength in her hands.

Back in June, we were told by a team of doctors at United Hospital, *She has two to four months left.* We were told, *Bring her home and make her as comfortable as you can.*

I remember my mom trying not to cry. Surrounding her hospital bed, the rest of us cried. We couldn't hide it from her. Even when some of us tried, crying instead in the hospital's family waiting room at the end of the hallway, she still heard us.

We took her home the next day. Spurred by the news that she had several months left to live, my mom dispatched her sister, sisters-in-law, brothers, and brother-in-law to make Lao beef jerky. She didn't call them right away. She waited about a week before picking up the phone. During that time, we turned my finished basement into my parents' apartment. We rearranged the furniture, pushing the sectional into the corner and making it into a permanent pullout bed for my mom.

When Akiem and I first got engaged, Mom insisted that we begin wedding planning. She didn't care about decor, the reception site, the wedding date, or even my traditional Lao wedding dress. She wanted only two things: 1) to invite the thirty to forty of her friends who she guaranteed would gift us a minimum of a hundred dollars each, and 2) to have full curation of our dinner menu, with Lao beef jerky being a nonnegotiable appetizer. For the Lao, the tradition of serving beef jerky with sticky rice at weddings spans back many generations. The belief is that by providing a hard-to-come-by protein at an auspicious occasion, the bride and groom are forging a path for good fortune to enter their home. The cow for the Lao is like the rambutan for Lao Americans in the eighties and nineties.

Akiem and I never got to have the wedding reception my mom wanted. We saved up money to buy the house on Rivoli Street instead.

My aunt Khamsone (my father's younger sister) moved in with us in the middle of June to help take care of my mom. She has a rotund build, a wide smile, boy-cut hair that never grays, and bunions on both feet that she's very proud of. She wears her feelings on her sleeve and is my clapback mentor. I was relieved to have her with us. She was living alone across town in one of the high-rises by Como Lake. Our family knows that lake as The Place Where We Foraged for Snails While White People Jogged Past Us. I knew it as The Lake That I Pretended I Jogged Around During Volleyball Practice. I don't remember which one of us picked up my aunt from her high-rise, but the day she moved in she came with two overnight bags, a Caboodle of her medications and perfumes, and a set of fuzzy, heavy-as-fuck Korean blankets—one with roses, one with a smiling tiger. She insisted on sleeping on the thick shag rugs on the floor next to the television, parallel to the sofa bed, even though my dad ordered her to sleep in their bedroom. She slept there until the end.

Uncle Ping Pong—real name Vieng (my father's younger brother by twenty years)—was a butcher at one of the Hmong slaughterhouses in town. I never asked him how he came to get that name, but I knew that either one of his Cretin-Derham Hall classmates gave it to him or one of his fellow refugee homies did. He wasn't a ping-pong athlete. He's a spritely man with a small, athletic frame. He didn't resemble a ping-pong ball or ping-pong paddle or ping-pong table or even a ping-pong net. Whatever the reason, I've always found his nickname to be ambiguously racist, as if his classmates smashed the phrase "ching chong" together with their stereotype of Asian ping-pong players and got—my uncle.

Uncle Ping Pong was ordered by Aunt Khamsone to bring home cuts of meat because Mom had a craving for Lao beef jerky. And Uncle Ping Pong did. The first night he came over with a little over ten pounds of beef. Aunt Khamsone got to work. She found the cutting board, the sharpest knife, the largest metal bowl, and the kitchen floor (also known as a Lao cook's comfort place). She sliced the first boulder of meat into fifty to seventy thin slabs. When she was done with that, she slapped another boulder of red marbled meat on the cutting board and sliced another set of sixty to eighty slabs. *Thick enough so it doesn't break like a cracker but thin enough so that you just flash-fry it,* she said.

When I was younger, I used to lie on the grass next to my mom and my aunts after they'd harvested the sun-dried beef slabs from the tower of Lao beef jerky drying on window screens in the backyard. Sometimes parts of jerky would stick to the wire screen. They'd laugh and say, *Alms for the flies. We are such giving people! We will be blessed in the next life!* They sorted the dehydrated sheets of meat into ziplock bags. Every now and then, I'd sift through the metal bowls to find the thinnest slice and hold it up into the sky, blocking the sun, like it was some sort of stained glass to be used in a mosaic later. They'd never shoo me away even though I'd stall the process. They were just glad that any of the kids took interest in doing Lao anything.

I had three key jobs at the Lao beef jerky factory at Rivoli. The first was to open the jar of white MSG flakes (foodies know this as umami; Lao know it as nua) and the canister of pink sea salt. The second was to peel and mince the garlic, ginger, and lemongrass. The third was to lay the meat onto the food dehydrator trays.

When prompted, I would sift the jar and the canister until it rained MSG and salt onto my aunt's hands. *MSG to enhance the taste,* she said. *Salt to preserve the juiciness of the meat.* I enjoyed watching her massage the seasonings and minced garlic, lemongrass, and ginger into the meat. I loved hearing the squishing of meat juices. I could smell the garlic, the lemongrass, my aunt's sweat, and the Liz Claiborne perfume she bathes in every morning, an amalgamated scent I've renamed "Seen Hanng Lao Eau de Parfum" or Lao Beef Jerky Perfume.

How to Make Lao Beef Jerky

Ingredients:
1 pound thinly sliced meat (flank preferred, but use whatever you have)
a few cloves garlic, finely chopped
1 stalk lemongrass, finely finely finely chopped
1 thumb ginger, finely chopped
1 tablespoon salt
1 tablespoon MSG (if you're brave and don't believe the racist
    lies about MSG)
splash light soy sauce

Tools:
1 sharp knife
1 large metal bowl
1 cutting board
1 sister-in-law
1 daughter
1 brother-in-law
a generous slaughterhouse
a food dehydrator

Directions:
Massage all of the ingredients in the bowl. Laugh at your aunt's dumb jokes and the stories she's telling you about the pathetic men who said she was "too much trouble" because she was good at saying "no" and insisting she didn't need some boy from the village. You could let

the meat marinate in a Tupperware container in the fridge overnight, or you could lay out the meat on the food dehydrator trays right away. Does it matter? What's the hurry? There is no rush to finish this task. Turn the temperature to whatever the manual for the food dehydrator tells you to for "meat." Wait six hours. Maybe more? Don't sit and wait for it. Go to bed. When the machine has dinged and you've lifted off the top, have ziplock bags ready. Stuff the dried jerky into the bags. Collect them into the large metal mixing bowl your mom bought you as a housewarming present. Bring her the bowl of jerky-filled ziplock bags and exclaim, *You could eat this every day for years, Mom, and you'll never run out.*

Watch her smile. Smile back. Turn around and walk the bowl to the chest freezer that lives in your laundry room. Gently arrange the bags so they will all fit. When you feel a craving coming on, you can flash-fry or bake the jerky. It's nonnegotiable that you prepare a bamboo basket of freshly steamed sticky rice. You are a luk khao niew, after all. Live up to your starch lineage, Descendent of Sticky Rice.

Start this process all over again when Uncle Ping Pong brings home another Igloo cooler full of meat from the Hmong slaughterhouse.

When you eat the Lao beef jerky, you will realize Mom was directing your aunts and uncles on how to take care of you after you bury her. Without saying it, Mom was confessing, *I'm worried that your father will starve when I am gone. How will he eat Lao food when I am not here?*

. . . .

Saymoukda Duangphouxay Vongsay is a Lao American poet and playwright. Her poetry appears in journals, magazines, anthologies, and more. Her plays have been presented by the Smithsonian Asian Pacific American Center, Theater Mu, Lower Depth Theatre, and other venues. She is an Andrew W. Mellon Playwright in Residence, McKnight Foundation Fellow, and Jerome Hill Artist Fellow.

Taking Langar: Ancestral Blueprints for Mutual Aid and Abolition

· · · · · · · · · · · · · · · ·

Simi Kang

"Care is the antidote to violence."

> —Saidiya Hartman, speaking at In the Wake:
> A Salon in Honor of Christina Sharpe

While I have left my hometown, Bde Óta Othúŋwe (the Dakota name for so-called Minneapolis), many times, I have never missed home more than in the last few months. Since May 25, 2020, I have cheered my chosen family on as they've paved the way for an ongoing local and global uprising in support of the Movement for Black Lives and for the abolition of policing in all forms.[1]

I have also watched as already underserved community members are hit hardest by a political imperative to do harm, be it refusing to contain a deadly virus that overwhelmingly kills members of the BIPOC community, sending more police to shut down uprisings in major cities, or the ongoing horrors of the food system for migrant workers and refugees. When communities find themselves in crisis—for revolution, compounded by a global pandemic, presents its own crises—housing, health care, and food are most tenuous. Maintaining all three requires our

---

[1] An earlier version of this essay appeared in Unmargin: Asian Americans Challenging, Encouraging, Educating, August 24, 2020, https://www.unmargin.org/takinglangar.

See the syllabus from the Toronto Abolition Convergence 2020 for excellent resources on abolition.

communities to build sustainable networks of care, or mutual aid, to help one another where the powers that be refuse to.[2]

For me, doing mutual aid in the uprising has meant seeking ways to effectively engage in it as a part of my daily life. Since June 1, I have been a part of the Twin Cities Mutual Aid Project (TCMAP), represented by an online map of almost three hundred sites providing food, personal care items, legal support, and so on across the Twin Cities metro. I contribute via Zoom and Slack from my home in Dionde:gâ (the Seneca name for what is called Pittsburgh), joining the hundred-plus volunteers who are working to maintain their communities' health and futures through mutual aid. For many Indigenous, Black, and other folks of color, this work is neither new nor uprising-specific—what is being called mutual aid today is bone-deep knowledge we have undertaken out of love and necessity.

As COVID and the uprising have made people's daily lives more and more tenuous, I have returned to the things my dadiji (paternal grandmother in Punjabi, the language spoken by my Indian family members) taught me about care; she showed me the value of making extra food for neighbors, that childcare is a communal project, and that everyone you share space with is family.[3] Through unpacking these ancestral blueprints for care, I am realizing that while community care has always been imperative for our (colonized, immigrant, refugee, migrant) survival at home and in diaspora, it has also been the underpinning of our ancestors' and our own rebellion in the name of survival. The Twin Cities uprising—and so many that have come before it—is

---

[2] On mutual aid, see Big Door Brigade, "What Is Mutual Aid?"

[3] I am the daughter of a white Minnesotan mother and Punjabi Sikh immigrant father. I grew up middle class on Dakota and Ojibwe land in Mni Sóta Maḳoce, called Minnesota (see Daḳota Wicohaŋ, Mni Sóta Maḳoce Curriculum), where I often pass as white. In addition to these privileges, I am a working scholar with a PhD. I have moved a great deal to do research, and have taken jobs financed by land grant and other settler, capitalist institutions on the traditional lands of many Indigenous communities.

such a rebellion, highlighting for many how mutual aid is imperative for and co-constitutive of all revolutionary movements, including the current US movement for police abolition.

Watching folks create new possibilities for themselves and their loved ones under explicit and rampant oppression has made me wonder what ancestral knowledge we can each bring to bear in this moment. More explicitly, what can our ancestors, as diverse and differently compelled as they are, tell us is the path forward in the impossible moments and the impossibly possible ones we continue to find ourselves in? For me, a white-passing mixed Sikh midwesterner, this looks like unpacking Sikhism's lessons for both rebellion and care.

On a cold night in October 2018, I stood outside my favorite South Asian restaurant in Bde Óta Othúŋwe, dancing to keep warm as I waited for my friend to join me. The plan was to eat as much onion bujia (fritters) and baingan bharta (stewed, roasted eggplant) as possible before heading to Hidden Falls for Barebones, an annual fall celebration in the spirit of Día de los Muertos and Samhain. After settling in, my friend took off their coat to reveal a deep green sweatshirt. I smiled, taking in the word "abolitionist," which was stamped across their chest in big white block letters.

We'd met in the fall of 2017 at a convening called Abolish Border Imperialism!, where the abolition of policing and colonialism was at the top of everybody's minds. At the opening plenary, Nick Estes presented his ongoing work for Native American sovereignty and demilitarization.[4] He was followed by Ricardo Levins Morales, a local Puerto Rican artist and activist, who talked about a collective that imagined a police-free future for Minneapolis: MPD150.[5] For twenty minutes, Levins Morales stood in front of

---

[4] Dhillon and Estes, "Introduction: Standing Rock, #NoDAPL, and Mni Wiconi"; Estes, *Our History Is the Future.*
[5] Walsh, "Activist Poster Artist Ricardo Levins Morales."

a packed auditorium and explained that police do not protect us. Rather, he said, we should redistribute the Minneapolis Police Department's budget to schools, social services provisioning, housing, and other resources that fundamentally allow Twin Cities residents to care for themselves and one another without surveillance, profiling, and punitive harm.

At our dinner a year later, my friend and I talked about their recent involvement in MPD150 and abolition work. They told me about folks like Ruth Wilson Gilmore, Dean Spade, and Mariame Kaba, explaining that abolition was not disbanding the police in a single moment. Instead, it is a process of defunding them over time while reallocating their budgets to things that would actually keep us safe—things we have been fighting for for generations to safeguard our youth and elders against violence, trauma, and harm.[6]

As we neared the end of dinner, my friend told me that the scariest part of abolition was that most folks couldn't imagine what happens after policing.[7] This is because, according to Kaba, "as a society, we have been so indoctrinated with the idea that we solve problems by policing and caging people that many cannot imagine anything other than prisons and the police as solutions to violence and harm."[8] My friend rejected this notion. "*We're* already replacing police," they said, waving their index finger between the two of us emphatically. "We already know how to take care of each other. It's called mutual aid."[9]

This was the first time I heard the term *mutual aid*, which refers to the collective, collaborative work that disabled people, BIPOC, queer, trans, and two-spirit people, women, immigrants, migrants, refugees, colonized people, and members of so many

---

[6] Berger, Kaba, and Stein, "What Abolitionists Do."
[7] That is, militarism, border regulation, immigrant and BIPOC detention, imperialism, settler colonialism, other ongoing colonialisms, and more.
[8] Kaba, "Yes, We Literally Mean Abolish the Police."
[9] Just Recovery, "What Is Mutual Aid?"

other structurally underserved communities do to keep ourselves alive.[10] Scooping up more eggplant with a piece of chapati,
I thought about my dadiji, who had made this dish for me so many
times. Savoring that bite, I realized that the concept of mutual aid
and its corollary, abolition, were legible to me from my earliest
memories with my father's family: "I think Sikhs do mutual aid
too, especially with food."

My dadiji was a devout Sikh. As a child, I did not have other Punjabis in my daily life. But on annual trips with my father to our
family farm in India, I learned about who we were—as Kangs, as
Punjabis, and as Sikhs. On those visits, Dadiji took me along on
her almost-daily trips to our local gurdwara, where Sikhs wor-
ship. Each ritual—walking barefoot on cold white marble, wash-
ing my hands under a communal spigot, giving an offering in
front of the Granth, and eating prashad blessed by the gyanis—
was precious to me. But my favorite part of going to gurdwara
was when we took langar, the two times daily, vegetarian communal meal served free to all.[11]

After praying, Dadiji and I would head to a long hall where
we'd sit on the floor. Nestled next to other eaters at the pangat
(long strips of cotton cloth that serve as "tables"), she would in-
struct me to hold up my tin plate for the sewadars as they paced
from person to person with efficient grace. As they walked down
the line one after another, each dipped a large ladle into a bucket
full of raita, channa, dal, or sabzi before gently placing its contents on our plates. As we ate, I watched this ritual repeated over
and over as newcomers joined us and others ate second and third
servings at the sewadars' urging. Everyone got what they needed.

---

[10] Flanders, "Mutual Aid Justice: Beyond Survival."
[11] As I show later, gurdwaras are not the only places where langar occurs. They
are just the most common. Langar is a part of annual celebrations and takes
place where it is needed, including outdoors and as a delivery service during
COVID-19.

At my family's gurdwara, langar was never a somber meal. My dadiji would say hi and joke with whomever was sitting next to us, often someone she had met on a prior visit. I loved watching these exchanges; while I never fully understood the Punjabi that melodically tripped out of everyone's mouths, these meals were early lessons in how to build community: share a meal, share a space—share a little more each time.

Taking langar with my dadiji fundamentally shaped how I conceive of my place in the world. At the age of four or five, I was starting to understand that being Sikh meant being part of a global family. As I grew up, I learned that this family was formed from and shaped by resistance to oppression, be it via a structural lack of food or, in so many cases, outright harm. What makes me most proud of my heritage is the fact that, while our families have lived through persistent persecution, Sikhs have always responded by making it our work to do what we call seva ("selfless service"), providing care for and with everyone selflessly and relentlessly. For my father's family, care and resistance are one and the same.[12]

Since George Floyd was murdered and the third MPD precinct was taken by protestors in the Twin Cities, residents of Dionde:gâ (Pittsburgh) have stayed in the streets fighting for Black lives.[13] They are fighting for structurally harmed Black trans people,

---

[12] That persecution includes genocide, as carried out by the Indira and Rajiv Gandhi governments in 1984. Ideas, "It's Time India Accept Responsibility for Its 1984 Sikh Genocide."

It is critical to acknowledge that while I am speaking from a Sikh and mixed-white framework, Indigenous and Black women and trans and nonbinary folks, whose expertise I overwhelmingly invoke throughout, have built the foundations on which all of my analysis rests. Additionally, as UnMargin editor Dr. Vidhya Shanker reminded me, while this is where my analysis rests, it does not mean that other communities that I do not evoke here, for example, Dalit scholars and activists, haven't been thinking through care work and community support for generations.

[13] Aizura, "A Mask and a Target Cart."

women, and queer folks, including Jonny Gammage, Tony Mc-Dade, and Nina Pop. They are also fighting for the lives of Black youth like Antwon Rose II, who was murdered by East Pittsburgh police on June 19, 2018.

I have largely watched this history unfold from my apartment, just a few blocks from the Tree of Life * Or L'Simcha synagogue, where a white nationalist terrorist shot eleven Jewish congregants in October 2018 and where the doors remain closed. I have felt deeply inspired as organizers tirelessly assert their own demands for Black futures and the abolition of policing here. In the wake of the police murder of Black community members and ongoing acts of xenophobia both nationally and locally, the Movement for Black Lives is life-affirming for all residents of Pittsburgh.

At the same time, my heart has ached for home. For months now, I have been galvanized by young people fighting tear gas and flash-bang grenades for their right not just to survival but also to a future.[14] Have been enlivened as community members also have, in light of months of long-standing, COVID-amplified vulnerabilities. Have wanted to support folks who struggled to care for themselves and their loved ones as grocery stores, transit, and other resources have become more tenuous or disappeared entirely.

In late May, mutual aid groups sprang up on Facebook to support neighborhoods across the Twin Cities. They were designed to provide forums for residents to share resources and understand where to find housing or diapers, transportation, pharmacies, and most persistently, food. Browsing the "South Minneapolis" group in late May, I found a map that was updated in real time, indicating whether grocery stores, convenience stores, and other imperative spaces were damaged, open, or closed. The map also listed modified store hours and indicated

[14] "George Floyd Uprising," Unicorn Riot.

whether a store was open for the foreseeable future or was taking it day by day. I reached out to the folks who built this map and, for two weeks, joined other volunteers every morning to cold-call twenty or forty of hundreds of stores to see if they were able to meet their neighborhood's needs.

Thankfully, the grocery store map became redundant in early June, when stores that were not damaged quickly reopened and kept regular hours. But the return of spaces where folks could trade money for food did not solve the economic devastation of COVID-19. It did not solve uncertain housing and lack of rent and mortgage freezes, or the food apartheid that is rampant across the Twin Cities metro area and the United States.[15] These compounding violences are not just exacerbated by policing but are also the direct results of it. As Dakota writer Diane Wilson (citing an elder) reminds us in *A Good Time for the Truth: Race in Minnesota*: "If you control the food, you can control the people."[16]

As I have said, the Sikh edict and practice of relentless care is my ancestral link to mutual aid. As Bay Area chef, organizer, and founder of JustUS Kitchen Jocelyn Jackson recently told Soleil Ho: "These traditions [of mutual aid] have been handed down for generations. Not because we know how to do it better, but because it was necessary for our survival. And it's really, really beautiful to see our instincts play out today from a place that is ancient, because one of the first things you do in a crisis—that I've learned both overtly and also just through practice—is that you caretake for the folks that are most at risk first." This caretaking, as Jack-

---

[15] Grinstein-Weiss, et al., "Housing Hardships Reach Unprecedented Heights During the COVID-19 Pandemic"; Olson, "Food Justice"; Civil Eats Editors, "After a Decade of Food Access Work, Are People Eating Any Healthier?"; Wyatt, "Finding Hope & Resilience During Challenging Times."
[16] Diane Wilson, "Seeds for Seven Generations," in Shin, ed., *A Good Time for the Truth*, 215.

son emphasizes and as my experiences of taking langar confirm, has most often been done through food.[17]

Because Sikhs have faced persecution throughout our histories, mandating interpersonal care and care for all is a survival tactic, a compassionate practice emerging from violence, a way to resist the violence of structural inequality and insecurity. Langar was one such practice. Established in the seventeenth century, it has always been used to provide nutritious, culturally relevant food to anyone living with food insecurity and/or under food apartheid.

Long before COVID, national and global Sikh groups like the Sikh Coalition and Khalsa Aid were providing langar, respectively, within their US communities and as a service to refugees and communities impacted by disaster globally. Since COVID-19 stay-at-home orders began, these same organizations have been offering daily langar in creative ways, including hosting drive-up events at gurdwaras, regularly taking pizza to hospitals to sustain health care workers on twenty-four-hour shifts, and ensuring that people forced to live in inter- and intranational refugee camps have prepared meals.

Given langar's place in both care and resistance work, I wasn't surprised to see that Sikhs' commitment to community food provisioning has only grown in the uprising. This is evidenced in many articles, including Priya Krishna's *New York Times* piece "How to Feed Crowds in a Protest or Pandemic? The Sikhs Know." After unpacking langar's history and speaking with members of gurdwaras and other Sikh community spaces across the United States, Krishna turns to the uprising, asking community members why they have created outdoor spaces near protests and/or opened their doors to protestors.

I cried as I read the piece, particularly enlivened by the

---

[17] Ho and Phillips, "How JustUs Kitchen Feeds the Movement."

answer a young Kaur studying at University of California, Irvine, gave to Krishna: "It is our duty to stand up with others to fight for justice. . . . Langar at its core is a revolution—against inequality and the caste system."[18] In the current context, langar is not abstract resistance; it is abolition work. Replacing violent structures (stratification systems and caste oppression, among others) with ones that respond to community-identified needs is explicitly a path away from persecution. As Kaur says, serving others selflessly to meet their needs *is* a revolution, but this service, clearly, is not just done through food. It is done by freely and reciprocally sharing one's resources, be that time, knowledge, skill, or thing, to fortify one's own community, something I became more aware of as I dove deeper into the Twin Cities mutual aid landscape.

In early June, I discovered that a much more complex map had emerged as grocery stores reopened: the Twin Cities Mutual Aid Project (TCMAP). This new map was a direct response to the massive mobilization of community members who had converted storefronts, churches, parking lots, and many other spaces into sites distributing food, personal care items, clothing, and other community needs in the days and weeks following George Floyd's murder. From the first week of June on, over a hundred folks brought together their heterogeneous skills, including programming, data entry, storytelling, education, and so on, to build and maintain a map of many of the burgeoning mutual aid sites throughout the Twin Cities metro area.[19]

My role is in data entry; when a site has new needs for ice, diapers, etc., they reach us in two ways. Sites either tell a peer on our "street team," whose members stay in touch with mutual aid

---

[18] Krishna, "How to Feed Crowds in a Protest or Pandemic? The Sikhs Know." A founding principle of Sikhism is the eradication of inequality and the caste system, which our founder, Guru Nanak, understood as going hand in hand.
[19] Mancall-Bitel, "Mutual Aid Groups Band Together to Feed Communities Through Crisis."

sites, or they reach us via technological means: messaging us on Facebook, emailing us, or texting. As the information comes in, we add it to the map, which updates in real time so that residents can contribute to site requests or get their needs met quickly. While grocery stores opened within a week or two of the primary uprising in late May and early June, inequality, capitalism, neo-liberalism, and COVID-19 have made it impossible for most Twin Cities residents to comfortably or easily access basic needs.

Because many mappers' families and loved ones understand that managing communities has always provided the blueprints for urban structural violence since settlement, we know that the Twin Cities have never been "the most livable place" for the ma-jority of us or our communities.[20] We mappers see every day that what community members are doing on the ground to "fill the gap" of pre-uprising services (from housing to mental health) is not a return to normal. Instead, it is a push toward a more local-ized, interpersonal future.[21]

By trying to amplify these dreams-made-tangible, TCMAP hopes we can provide support, connection, and reciprocity for many of the folks doing the grounded, exhausting, and heart-full work of imagining otherwise.[22] As such, our essential purpose is to better facilitate care—if someone needs something, they can see what their community is offering nearby; if someone wants to give, they can find where community members have a need; and if critical structures, like temporary, organized responses to

---

[20] Minneapolis has made many "best of" lists in terms of quality of life, cycling culture, etc.

[21] Agyeman, "Urban Planning as a Tool of White Supremacy"; Holder, "Why This Started in Minneapolis."

I again thank Dr. Shanker for offering a great deal of complexity to this idea in her review comments. I am choosing to replicate them here because I can't say it any better: "neoliberalism matters here, I think, too—that the neoliberal state has essentially been abdicating/outsourcing/privatizing its responsibility to black and brown peoples while subsidizing the care and growth of white folks in the suburbs, etc."

[22] Grandoit, "Adrienne Maree Brown on Creating the Future."

housing injustice, are being (re)imagined, they have folks to ask for support in real time.[23]

This approach to buttressing extant care networks fits comfortably into my favorite definition of mutual aid, from Big Door Brigade: "Mutual aid is when people get together to meet each other's basic survival needs with a shared understanding that the systems we live under are not going to meet our needs and we can do it together *right now!*"[24] Following these edicts for right engagement and community care, TCMAP understands itself as one tiny node of many in the aforementioned web of community members thinking in the near term to address resource insecurity over time.

This form of political participation, Big Door Brigade goes on to say, rejects the more common notions of charity (which is "often a strategy for controlling poor people") and social services (part of the nonprofit industrial complex, wherein "rich people and corporations get to decide what strategies should be funded").[25] Dr. Vidhya Shanker recently underscored this in a social media post, saying: "Charity is exploitation spelled backwards. Equally unsustainable. Equally unjust." Centering the needs and voices of people over profit and rejecting charity for actual engagement are explicitly abolitionist acts. As Ruth Wilson Gilmore has said, "Abolition is about presence, not absence. It's about building life-affirming institutions."[26] By doing mutual aid, Twin Cities residents are affirming their and their neighbors' lives be-

---

[23] See Minneapolis Sanctuary Movement, https://minneapolissanctuary.org/.

[24] Big Door Brigade, "What Is Mutual Aid?"

[25] Incite, "Beyond the Non-Profit Industrial Complex." To my mind, this "strategy for controlling poor people" is specifically because charity maintains the status quo, where resourced people "give" to structurally underserved people, but not in ways that change the structures that produce class, race, disability, gender, and so many other structural violences. Charity requires these structures to stay as they are; it wants few people to maintain power over many.

[26] Quoted in Herskind, "Some Reflections on Prison Abolition."

cause, if the police are to be abolished, community care will be what we have left.[27]

As I said early on, "abolition" and "mutual aid" have truly become everyday language in the Twin Cities and elsewhere as the massive and ongoing movement for life and against oppression continues to grow. Like my dadiji showed me so long ago, TCMAP is highlighting for me that care is not just central to our daily lives but imperative to abolition.

Sikhs have effectively been doing what is called mutual aid since the foundation of our faith. My global family's "institutional" knowledge of how to feed people, be it finding the funds to do so or the ability to churn out gallons of tasty, culturally appropriate, and healthful food for and by community members, is, I think, particularly compelling for our ongoing reckoning with policing, anti-Blackness, violence against Indigenous communities (especially women and girls), white supremacy, and fascism. As Krishna's interviewees showed, when we feed each other, we are not simply saying, "here, eat well"; we are actively producing futures in places where the future has been foreclosed.

At the same time, it is important to make clear that mutual aid is not utopian but egalitarian work; it arises and is sustained via a myriad of complex, meandering, and iterative approaches. It is messy, and there are likely more ways to get it wrong than there are to do it well. Moving away from the structures that bind us is not easy—there is never agreement, predictability, or safety as we stumble our way through and against massive change. But if

---

[27] While the outward function of TCMAP is to bridge resources and needs in our communities, like other mutual aid projects, many of its volunteers have a parallel dedication to taking wealth out of spaces of power (policing, prisons, the military) and redistributing it to spaces that actively support and maintain community (schools, libraries, health care, etc.). This dual commitment is how mutual aid and abolition are linked—each requires the other, and those who facilitate one are often creating the framework for the other.

we follow the path of abolition, taking one intentional yet force-ful step at a time, it might be possible to create community that looks, feels, sounds, and even tastes drastically different. Different from acquiescing to state-mandated Black and Indigenous death; from schools acting as pipelines to prison; from disabled family being refused the resources they need to survive. Different from daily insecurities as the norm for huge numbers of our community and chosen, natal, and queer kin.[28]

Creating community that embodies these differences is pos-sible in large part because life-after-abolition is determined by those with the most to lose if it falls apart rather than by those who have the most to gain from communities' and cities' ongoing abjection: politicians, the military and carceral industrial com-plexes, and corporations writ large. When we care for each other, we actively reject the structures that require our harm to main-tain themselves (capitalism, ableism, militarism, xenophobia, imperialism, casteism, settler colonialism, racism, transphobia, and on and on). We are taking them out of the equation as much as possible, and instead of using goods and needs to produce more power, we are decentralizing power and wealth by moving resources where they are needed.

This is hard work under neoliberalism and capitalism; it re-quires a fair amount of security to think beyond one's own im-mediate needs and, too, requires a number of resources to extend out to others. At the same time, mutual aid and abolition ask that

---

[28] I again thank Dr. Shanker for adding thoughtful complexity to the notion of kin (for more about the various ways we can imagine kin, I suggest reading scholarship by Shanker herself, Zoe Todd, Robin Wall Kimmerer, June Jordan, Audre Lorde, bell hooks, Psyche Williams-Forson, and so many more; con-suming art by Studio Revolt, Saymoukda Duangphouxay Vongsay, Sham-e-Ali Nayeem, Bao Phi, Chaun Webster, Sun Yung Shin, Lisa Marie Brimmer, Hieu Minh Nguyen, Patricia Smith, Cece Carpio, Ocean Vuong, and so many others; and learning about the work of collectives like the People's Kitchen Collective, New Orleans–based Women with a Vision and Antenna, and many, many more.

those who benefit from systems of violence offer those benefits to others. This extension does not abolish capitalism or attendant structures like racism in any way. It does, however, allow us to think of capital differently[29]: if I have more—time, money, mental health, physical health, people in my networks, social capital, etc.—I use those things for the benefit of my community rather than keeping them for me alone. Because ultimately these are not the only types of wealth—they are simply the kinds we have been forced to value.[30]

If my communities are resourced, our collective future is inherently more resourced, and we can begin unweaving cycles of deprivation, violence, and pain from our everyday experiences. As Leah Lakshmi Piepzna-Samarasinha told me, "[disabled folks] and poor moms are the real OGs of mutual aid and we know how to do it . . . because we get why care is both skilled work and vulnerable." We do not resist systems to re-create them—we resist them to make something else entirely.

To do this, we must foundationally retrain our neural pathways to see care as both skilled and highly valued work. We must reject patriarchal ideas about feeling and caring so we can center vulnerability, empathy, and interpersonal connection in building new communities. Mutual aid is not easy, but it is essential. If we reject the neoliberal ideal of centering our own (consumer) needs at the expense of everyone else and instead honor our interrelation with the people and more-than-human beings within and

---

[29] I say this knowing full well that the specter of capital has been thought about differently by an extensive number of theorists, activists, and revolutionaries, a small snapshot of which includes Karl Marx, Cedric Robinson, Huey Newton, Bobby Seale, Malcolm X, Fred Moten, Grace Lee Boggs, Larry Itliong, Dolores Huerta, César Chávez, Iyko Day, Aimee Bahng, Nick Estes, Adam Bledsoe, and Jodi Melamed.

[30] Listen to Leah Lakshmi Piepzna-Samarasinha's discussion of "crip wealth" on the Disability Visibility Project (Episode 48: "Care Work," April 7, 2019) for an example of wealth that refuses capitalist norms and regulations.

beyond the borders we wish to dismantle, we can begin to move toward a culture based in reciprocity and care.[31]

When we receive and give support, we resist. When we receive and give support, we build collective futures. When we receive and give support, we abolish systems that never meant for us to survive, anyway.

· · · · · · · · ·

Postscript: In late September 2020, Sikhs' relationship with food, resistance, and mutual aid became global news. Narendra Modi's government pushed through three farm bills that will economically devastate India's already struggling farmers by depriving them of price assurance and, thus, security. Since then, farmers have protested by blocking major roadways across the nation, including into Delhi.

The #FarmersProtest is led by Sikhs, who have always resisted colonial and national attacks on our community's primary livelihood. As the Delhi shutdown continues, farming families have set down roots. They make seva daily, building shelters for elders, supplying free stores full of necessities, and giving langar to all. After major protests on January 26, 2021, Modi's government beat and jailed two hundred people, including elders, and cut internet, power, and water to protest sites. In response, Sikh service organizations built lavatories and trucked in water. Then, they planted flowers beside metal spikes and barbed wire erected to contain them.

But this prison can't hold our kin. Men who look like my dadaji cook, dance, and sing together; women who look like my dadiji

---

[31] Pellow, "Critical Environmental Justice"; Krieger, "Abolish ICE, and Abolish the Border Too."

Again, I am not the first person to think about these things by any stretch of the imagination; for a much more thorough analysis, read work by radical disabled organizers and artists like the Sins Invalid (sinsinvalid.org) collective and critical disability thinkers like Mimi Khúc, Sami Schalk, Leroy Moore, Diana Louis, Margaret Price, Alice Wong, and Candace Coleman.

lead protests, fight for protestors who have been jailed, and mend clothing. They are called terrorists by their government. And they fight. This is the beauty of my people: for farmers, like leaders of the Movement for Black Lives, mutual aid is not a project, but a practice. I am scared for them every day, and I know they will win. This is because, as Saidiya Hartman reminds us, care is the antidote to violence. #IStandWithFarmers today and always. #KissanMazdoorEktaZindabaad

. . . .

Dr. Simi Kang is a Sikh American community advocate, educator, artist, and scholar. Her work centers Asian American collaborative resistance in the Gulf South, where folks are always imagining environmentally and economically just futures.

For Further Exploration

"Abolish Border Imperialism! A Convergence for Abolition and Decolonization." Conference. Twin Cities, MN, October 6–8, 2017. https://abolitionjournal.org/convergence2017/.

Agyeman, Julian. "Urban Planning as a Tool of White Supremacy— The Other Lesson from Minneapolis." The Conversation, July 27, 2020. https://theconversation.com/urban-planning -as-a-tool-of-white-supremacy-the-other-lesson-from -minneapolis-142249.

Aizura, Aren. "A Mask and a Target Cart: Minneapolis Riots." *The New Inquiry*, May 30, 2020. https://thenewinquiry.com/a-mask-and-a -target-cart-minneapolis-riots.

Berger, Dan, Mariame Kaba, and David Stein, "What Abolitionists Do." *Jacobin Magazine*, August 2017. https://www.jacobinmag .com/2017/08/prison-abolition-reform-mass-incarceration.

Big Door Brigade. "What Is Mutual Aid?" https://bigdoorbrigade.com/ what-is-mutual-aid.

Civil Eats Editors. "After a Decade of Food Access Work, Are People Eating Any Healthier?" Civil Eats, June 4, 2019. https://civileats .com/2019/06/04/after-a-decade-of-food-access-work-are-people -eating-any-healthier.

Daḳota Wicohaŋ. Mni Sóta Maḳoce Curriculum. https://dakotawicohan.org/courses/mni-sota-koce.

Dhillon, Jaskiran, and Nick Estes. "Introduction: Standing Rock, #NoDAPL, and Mni Wiconi." Society for Cultural Anthropology, December 22, 2016. https://culanth.org/fieldsights/introduction-standing-rock-no-dapl-and-mni-wiconi.

Disability Visibility Project. Episode 48: "Care Work." April 7, 2019. https://disabilityvisibilityproject.com/2019/04/07/ep-48-care-work.

Dixon, Ejeris, and Leah Lakshmi Piepzna-Samarasinha. "Mutual Aid Justice: Beyond Survival." *The Laura Flanders Show*, April 7, 2020. https://lauraflanders.org/2020/04/mutual-aid-justice-beyond-survival.

Estes, Nick. *Our History Is the Future: Standing Rock Versus the Dakota Access Pipeline, and the Long Tradition of Indigenous Resistance.* New York: Verso, 2019.

Flanders, Laura. "Mutual Aid Justice: Beyond Survival." *The Laura Flanders Show*, April 7, 2020. https://lauraflanders.org/2020/04/mutual-aid-justice-beyond-survival.

"George Floyd Uprising." Unicorn Riot. https://unicornriot.ninja/georgefloyd.

Grandoit, Alice. "Adrienne Maree Brown on Creating the Future." *Deem*, 2020. https://www.deemjournal.com/stories/amb.

Grinstein-Weiss, Michael, Brinda Gupta, Yung Chun, Hedwig Lee, and Mathieu Despard. "Housing Hardships Reach Unprecedented Heights During the COVID-19 Pandemic." Brookings, June 1, 2020. https://www.brookings.edu/blog/up-front/2020/06/01/housing-hardships-reach-unprecedented-heights-during-the-covid-19-pandemic.

Hartman, Saidiya. In the Wake: A Salon in Honor of Christina Sharpe, 2017. https://vimeo.com/203012536.

Herskind, Micah. "Some Reflections on Prison Abolition." December 7, 2019, https://micahherskind.medium.com/some-reflections-on-prison-abolition-after-mumi-5197a4c3cf98.

Herzing, Rachel. "Big Dreams and Bold Steps Toward a Police-Free Future." Truthout, September 16, 2015. https://truthout.org/articles/big-dreams-and-bold-steps-toward-a-police-free-future/.

Ho, Soleil, and Justin Phillips. "How JustUs Kitchen Feeds the Movement." *San Francisco Chronicle*, Extra Spicy podcast, July 13, 2020.

https://www.sfchronicle.com/food/article/Cook-activist-Jocelyn
-Jackson-uses-food-as-an-15391658.php.

Holder, Sarah. "Why This Started in Minneapolis." Bloomberg
CityLab, June 5, 2020. https://www.bloomberg.com/news/articles/
2020-06-05/revealing-the-divisive-history-of-minneapolis.

Ideas. "It's Time India Accept Responsibility for Its 1984 Sikh
Genocide." *Time*, October 31, 2014. https://time.com/3545867/
india-1984-sikh-genocide-anniversary.

Incite. "Beyond the Non-Profit Industrial Complex." https://incite
-national.org/beyond-the-non-profit-industrial-complex.

Just Recovery. "What Is Mutual Aid? A Primer by the Climate Justice Alliance." Climate Justice Alliance, July 13, 2020. https://
climatejusticealliance.org/what-is-mutual-aid-a-primer-by-the
-climate-justice-alliance.

Kaba, Mariame. "Yes, We Literally Mean Abolish the Police." *New York
Times*, June 12, 2020.

Khalsa Aid. https://www.khalsaaid.org/.

Krieger, Sonja. "Abolish ICE, and Abolish the Border Too: A Socialist
Perspective." Left Voice, July 30, 2018. https://www.leftvoice.org/
Abolish-Ice-and-Abolish-the-Border-Too-A-Socialist-Perspective.

Krishna, Priya. "How to Feed Crowds in a Protest or Pandemic? The
Sikhs Know." *New York Times*, June 8, 2020.

Maini, Tridivesh Singh. "36 Years Later, the Trauma of Operation Blue
Star Lingers On." Eleventh Column, June 7, 2020. https://www
.eleventhcolumn.com/2020/06/07/36-years-later-sikhs-continue
-to-remember-operation-blue-star-with-grief.

Mancall-Bitel, Nick. "Mutual Aid Groups Band Together to Feed
Communities Through Crisis." Eater, June 4, 2020. https://www
.eater.com/2020/6/4/21280367/mutual-aid-groups-food-donations
-george-floyd-protests.

Minneapolis Sanctuary Movement. https://minneapolissanctuary.org/.

The Movement for Black Lives. https://m4bl.org/.

MPD150. https://www.mpd150.com/about.

Olson, Norma Smith. "Food Justice: For LaDonna Redmond,
This Is the Civil Rights Issue of the 21st Century." Twin Cities
Daily Planet, June 4, 2013. https://www.tcdailyplanet.net/
food-justice-ladonna-redmond-civil-rights-issue-21st-century.

Pellow, David N. "Critical Environmental Justice." Pitzer College, October 18, 2019. https://www.youtube.com/watch?v=Hye4503gtkw.

Post, Todd. "Baltimore's Black Churches Take on Food Apartheid." Bread for the World, February 5, 2020. https://www.bread.org/blog/baltimores-black-churches-take-food-apartheid.

Reese, Ashante M. "Black Food Geographies in Washington, DC." Emory University, March 25, 2019. https://www.youtube.com/watch?v=ewH2Qamo31k.

Shin, Sun Yung, ed., *A Good Time for the Truth: Race in Minnesota*. St. Paul: Minnesota Historical Society Press, 2016.

The Sikh Coalition. https://www.sikhcoalition.org/.

SikhiWiki, Encyclomedia of the Sikhs. "Langar." https://www.sikhiwiki.org/index.php/Langar.

————. "Seva." https://www.sikhiwiki.org/index.php/Seva.

Sins Invalid. sinsinvalid.org.

Toronto Abolition Convergence. "An Indigenous Abolitionist Study Guide." Yellowhead Institute, August 10, 2020. https://yellowheadinstitute.org/2020/08/10/an-indigenous-abolitionist-study-group-guide.

Twin Cities Mutual Aid Project. https://tcmap.org/.

Walsh, Jim. "Activist Poster Artist Ricardo Levins Morales: 'It's Always about Supporting Resilience.'" MinnPost, February 18, 2019. https://www.minnpost.com/arts-culture/2019/02/activist-poster-artist-ricardo-levins-morales-its-always-about-supporting-resilience.

Wyatt, Lytisha. "Love Notes: Finding Hope & Resilience During Challenging Times." Soul Fire Farm, September 19, 2020. https://www.soulfirefarm.org/love-notes-finding-hope-resilience-during-challenging-times.

Home Is Where the Haleem Is

. . . .

Zarlasht Niaz

Food has a special way of expressing the things we can't say.

When I was in high school, I had my first real crush. It was the kind of crush that didn't fade. It kept growing and growing until it transformed into first love, but I couldn't tell him how I felt. Instead, I fed him.

I would wake early on school days, thirty minutes before my alarm, to get to the kitchen before everyone else was up. With groggy eyes, I would brew two cups of green tea with cardamom, mix green raisins with walnuts and dried chickpeas into little containers, and slip some of my mom's salty cookies into ziplock bags. I would take it all—chai sabz, kishmish o nakhut, kulche namaki—to school to share with him.

He was the first Afghan I had met who wasn't related to me. He had enrolled in my high school after coming to the United States alone from Kabul. We were the same color, except for his eyes, which were a bright greenish-yellow. He knew all of the songs on my lime green iPod Nano, and he pronounced my name right. Every morning, he would meet me by my locker to walk me to class, and every evening we texted each other for hours. I was enamored with him, but I never told him how I felt. I couldn't.

I didn't have the words to express what I wanted, I was scared of rejection, and, worst of all, I didn't have my parents' permission. My mom and dad barely approved of their daughters talking to boys; to become more than acquaintances was to breach the respect and obedience terms of our unspoken contract. Besides, how do you tell someone you have feelings for them if you're not allowed to date and you're too young to get married? *I can't hold your hand, but I really want to?*

I had learned from my mother that we can say *I love you* through our food, that each bite clarifies a singular truth: *you are loved.* Slouched against metal lockers in front of our class-rooms, waiting for our teachers to open their doors, we found a moment for something like love through a taste of home.

Of all of the things that tied my crush and me together, the strongest was our homesickness. His home had been Afghan-istan before he relocated here a couple of years prior. I was an Afghan American whose parents had left their homes in Afghan-istan in the 1980s, a decade before I was born. I had spent all of my life in the Midwest, yet it never felt like home. He was missing the home he had left behind, while I was missing a home I had not yet found.

I grew up in rural Wisconsin in a predominantly white town that was so small the state classified it as a village. When my family moved to a wealthy suburb of Minneapolis, it was racially much the same: homogenous and white. I was a brown, Muslim de-scendant of undocumented refugees attending predominantly white, Christian schools in a country where people like me were portrayed as backward, in need of saving from ourselves. The US government plays a significant and largely unacknowledged role in the suffering in my parents' homeland. How could I be at home here? But I had never lived in Afghanistan. How could I be at home there? Too Afghan for Americans and too American for Afghans, I felt out of place everywhere.

Starving for belonging, I searched for people who looked like me, knew the language I spoke at home, ate the foods I ate. But there were no Afghan community centers, bakeries, cafes, or gro-cery stores in the Midwest to escape to.

. . . .

There had always been a dissonance between how I understood Afghanistan and how it had been portrayed through the lens of militarization, as if we were all constructing the same puzzle but given different pieces. I knew Afghanistan through its dried fruits and nuts, its poetry, and its mountains, while everyone else seemed to see only its conflict. Recent military occupations of Afghanistan by the United States and by Soviet forces plunged the country into a period of war that started in the 1980s and has lasted more than forty years. As a result, Afghans would remain the largest population of refugees worldwide for thirty-two years. We are divided along social and ideological lines through our various ethnicities and political affiliations and along geographic borders of the countries we resettled in, yet I have understood food as a strong medium for unification. As Afghans, we often recognize home in the bright red threads woven into aqcha carpets as much as in the taste of the caramelized sugar that flavors qabli palao.

Afghan food is like the country itself—diverse and forever influencing and being influenced by its regional neighbors. As a landlocked country located in the "heart of Asia," Afghanistan's geographic centrality means many have passed through it; most famously travelers along the Silk Road crossed cities like Balkh and Kabul on their way to surrounding empires. These travelers exchanged food knowledge that influenced Afghan cuisine and shaped it into what it is today.

When as a child I dined out with my family, we would experience different elements of Afghan cuisine in various restaurants—curries in South Asian restaurants, dumplings in East Asian restaurants, kabobs in West Asian restaurants—and while these elements were similar to those found in Afghan food, they were never the same. Thanks to globalization, cuisines from all over the world are becoming more and more accessible to people everywhere. Yet I still struggle to find Afghan food in the Midwest.

If we had Afghan food at all, we either ate it most days for

dinner at home, or we had it at family parties courtesy of which-
ever poor khala had volunteered (or was volunteered by her husband) to cook. Living in the Midwest, I was limited to the kitchens
of family members, but don't get me wrong—the food coming
out of these kitchens was delicious. My mama made homemade
bread every week. My grandmother made the thickest, softest
rote. My aunts fed us creative renditions of mantu that replaced
the ground beef with mushrooms. Nevertheless, it was limiting
to only experience Afghan cuisine through my family members.
When the people around you don't know how to make something, it disappears from your plates and your memories.

In the Midwest, good Afghan food was usually a flight or two
away in big cities on the West or East Coast. California has the
largest population of Afghans in the United States. Fremont, California, is even called Little Kabul. When we'd visit, my family
would look forward to picking up naane tazah from local bakeries and bolani from the window of our favorite brick-and-mortar
shop. Where I grew up, Afghans often brand their restaurants as
"Middle Eastern" to market to midwesterners who wouldn't nec-
essarily recognize Afghan food. These restaurants' specialties
often become foods from other cultures, a fusion that produces
novelties like gyros flavored with Afghan spices and pizzas served
with chatni. But in California, Afghan restaurants are branded as
such, and their menus primarily comprise classic Afghan dishes.

California's Afghan food landscape retains a cultural memory
of home that is closer to what people have experienced in Afghanistan. Fremont's stores and restaurants, bakeries and sweetshops
feel like atomized cultural centers, vestiges of Afghan daily life
based on the memories of migrants who, for the most part, left
Afghanistan in the seventies and eighties.

Eating becomes an important way of transferring intergenerational knowledge and memory. When the children and
grandchildren of Afghan refugees eat the bolani and qabli palao
at these restaurants, we can imagine life as our parents and our

grandparents lived. We can imagine the country in which they grew up, the streets on which they played, and the food vendors from which they ate. This act of remembering and reconstructing is especially important for us as refugees because we often can't go home.

We, our children, and our grandchildren may never see Afghanistan, so we eat to remember.

The emptiness of the midwestern food landscape confined my exposure to Afghan food to specific events, experiences, and people. I don't have memories of ordering bolani during all-nighters with college friends, nor do I associate holidays with specific foods. Food was always a family experience, so relationships with family members often dictated how I related to our food. My mother fed us every day, usually home-cooked meals. She would cook for hours to fill our dastarkhan. No one could top my mom's cooking skills in presentation, abundance, or flavor.

The kitchen can also be a space that holds a lot of pain. As trauma around cooking hinders our connection to Afghan food, we no longer eat it to remember—we avoid it to forget.

Cooking was something I could never seem to do right. If my mother was cooking and I didn't offer to help, I was lazy. When I did offer to help, every move I made was a mistake. *Don't put the spoon on the counter; that's not clean. Why are you putting the plate so far from the pan? You're dripping oil everywhere. You come in the kitchen and make everything dirty. Instead of helping, you make my job harder. Just go. I will finish it by myself.*

I knew my mother fed me as a way to love me. She is an excellent cook. When we sat around the dining room table—my father at the head, my mother on his left side, and us children sitting around them—we'd be so grateful for her food. But I knew my role: I was meant to eat, not to cook.

Food is often integral to our relationship with our culture and identity as Afghan Americans, but developing healthy, affirming associations with our food is a privilege. If people have strained relationships with their caregivers or experience abuse from them, they may have a difficult time learning anything from them, including how to cook. Afghans have higher than average rates of mental illness, especially post-traumatic stress disorder, that often go untreated because of the stigma around mental health and the inaccessibility of mental health resources. This painful reality can take a large toll on parents and children in our communities. The kitchen can be a place for some to decompress, and it can be the opposite for others. For me, it became a space in which I was overwhelmed by unrealistic expectations of perfection and gendered stereotypes.

Thankfully tools exist that can help us engage with Afghan food in ways that are healthy and affirming. More and more recipes are becoming accessible online. On YouTube you can find videos in Dari so your grandma can watch, and videos in English so your non-Afghan friends can learn too. When I began using YouTube videos to cook, I had to grapple with the shame of feeling like I should have known how to make these foods because I grew up with a stay-at-home Afghan mom who cooked every day. It felt like I was cheating by watching these videos and learning from them. But I needed these videos because they allowed me to cook alone in an environment where I was comfortable.

The power dynamic between elders and young people can get in the way of the learning process. It makes it hard to try something new, as wavering from tradition and the advice of elders can be interpreted as disrespect. For some it is helpful to have an experienced person watching and giving them tips as they work, while for others it is more helpful to watch a video and learn on their own. For me, the important thing was to find what worked and to do it.

My first love didn't last. I never told him how I felt, and he moved on. We never went on a date or held hands or said "I love you." I didn't experience the hallmarks of an American love story—not that I wanted to—but I still had to endure the heartbreak. The end has a way of bringing you back to the beginning. I thought about everything we had shared, and it ended up being not very much. We were not a good match, but this truth had been clouded by the commonalities in our identity and how we understood home.

My first love, with all of its joy and sadness, taught me to stop looking for home in a boy. Or food. Or a geographic location. Home is me. I take it with me wherever I go. And our food reminds me of home because it reminds me of myself. The self that grew up stuffing aushak and balancing trays of tea for guests. Home is not about being around people who remind you of yourself. Home is where you feel accepted for being your full self. When I was hungering for my people, I was really hungering to be recognized, to be seen and to feel like there is space for me in this world. Somewhere where I don't have to change, or give up parts of myself, or compromise my right to my identity in order to live peacefully.

Finding home requires that we be ourselves publicly, that we express what we want and who we are. Our inner and outer worlds must meet. When we open Afghan restaurants in the United States, we are being ourselves publicly. When we reject the pressure of assimilation, we are being ourselves publicly. All of these actions require a great amount of vulnerability. Being the child of refugees can be painful. It can feel like your family is unwanted, pushed around with no control over your circumstances. When we bring our food with us and share it with the people around us, we take back some of that control. Being ourselves publicly gives others the opportunity to accept us. When we eat what we want and welcome others to do the same, we are making space for the belonging, acceptance, and love within community that we all crave.

Our food is our joy, our comfort, our safety—it represents everything that has been and continues to be jeopardized by the ongoing military occupations of Afghanistan. Our food's ability to migrate around the world with us is a testament to our resilience. Our way of life is alive and well. Our food is a living, breathing, evolving connection to Afghanistan and a manifestation of our collective memory. Through food we are able to pursue a sense of home that is beyond the limits of our environment, beyond the limits of the frustration we feel, the hopelessness and helplessness of living in a world where conflict controls so much of our lives.

As we build restaurants and grocery stores and cafes in the United States, we are establishing new roots. Regardless of whether we are welcomed to this country or not, whether we have papers or not, whether we are wanted or not—we are here. And these roots will continue to grow and carve out spaces for us where people never imagined we would be.

. . . .

Zarlasht Niaz is an Afghan American writer and organizer based in Minneapolis. She writes children's literature, poetry, and essays that center the experiences of Afghan American women and girls.

Lake Superior Looks Like the Ocean to Island Girls from Minnesota

. . . .

Junauda Petrus-Nasah

One

Ginger, lemon, honey, fresh thyme, orange peel, parsley, cilantro, cumin, sea salt, cracked black pepper. Curry. Lime. Sugar. Medicine is culinary, culinary is medicinal.

Two

This year I didn't grow a garden. Somehow I couldn't plant or nurture a thing beyond myself, and I did that barely. This year, my soul, body, and mind were a garden and all I had it in me to nurture. This summer kinda was weird from the jump; even though I felt the warmth coming in through the cracks of the pandemic, I was afraid to leave my home. We'd been home too much, too long; it was hard to imagine life before all of the captivity.

The first time I left my house to go anywhere besides the co-op or Target or a wistful walk around the neighborhood was the evening George Floyd was murdered. It happened a couple of blocks from my house, in front of a corner store that had called the cops on him, one that I had frequented to get rolling papers or coconut water. My homegirl, Andrea, had ridden her bike by my house on the way to check it out, and I decided to roll too.

That night I came home and sat on the couch and watched the city outside of my doors on CNN, while simultaneously hearing helicopters, police sirens, cars speeding, chanting, and loud pops. An uprising all around me. I am not sure if that is why I didn't garden and certainly could barely write. Every day was a hurricane of emotion, and every day was filled with organizing and meeting and doing work to keep my community healthy and sane. I was doing revolutionary work but in ways that felt far away from myself, from my altar the dirt. I was manic and depressed. I creeped into myself through dancing and kundalini yoga and sitting in the sun too. And staring out the window.

And as I write this, I feel a disappointment in myself. I wish I had it in me to grow food to eat in the middle of a pandemic and an uprising. I feel like I should be growing and canning like some of my revolutionary homies, and my ancestors, those versed in food systems and urban gardening. People who like me are suspicious of government. I know you shouldn't should on yourself. But how did they avoid being a puddle on the ground of life? And for long enough to do something so hopeful and sensible as plant a seed when the soil is ready? So instead, I insist that I gardened me this year. I planted and harvested little revolutions that live within myself and my ancestral memory.

Three

In the summers, my mom raised us kids gardening, like her grandfather taught her in Trinidad. My sisters hated it, but I loved it, especially weeding. Picking all of the useless-to-us green sprigs that would make way for a delicious earthy blackness, the color of crumbled Oreos. There are women who chew on dirt of red, black, and brown varieties, searching with tongue and mouth for the nutrients in the soil their bodies need. I loved the sweat and heat of being in our yard, nurturing and yielding soil and seed into food and herb. Medicine is culinary and culinary is medicinal; in gardens you feel the healing and the pleasure in herbs. My mom took pleasure in the nuanced perfection of a self-grown ingredient, how they tasted different than store-bought.

Four

My mom tells a story about Tantie Norma Pope, her great aunt in Trinidad. She owned a rum shop; had a face full of moles and a neck full of gold. Norma Pope is iconic for a lot of reasons. Never had her own kids but raised several. She had real money and property as a Black woman in the forties and fifties in the capital of Trinidad. My mom said she was one of a few women to have her own car, a big black car, solid. "I don't know what kind it was, but she had a car like Al Capone," my mom said, further mythologizing the warrior gangster, Norma Pope.

She raised the children of her sister who died during childbirth. One of those kids she raised was my grandfather, Kelvin. Norma Pope had another sister who died this way in England, and she sent for the newborn and two-year-old her sister left behind.

As a young woman, she began making her money selling doubles, a Caribbean street food made of fried bread, curry garbanzo beans, and tamarind sauce. It will literally change your life in the way simple foods do, like a slice of pizza, a taco, a dumpling, a samosa. Doubles is essential perfection with just fried dough and curried legumes and a drizzle of tangy tamarind sauce. She made her money by making doubles early in the morning and selling it to men who worked at the factories downtown.

One last thing I should mention about Tantie is she also was known to fight. Especially men if they harmed a woman; she would grow impatient with her brother's passivity in solving such matters and would settle it herself. "Norma Pope was a butt-er, yuh know?" I can hear my mom saying, talking about Tantie Norma Pope's signature move of headbutting her opponent.

Five

Tell me about your Trinidadian food ancestors. Over the years you would talk to me about your grandfather, your aunts, and what they taught you.

Thinking back now, I think I was greatly influenced by my mother's mother [Mabel] and my mother's father [Matthew]. As well as my father's aunt, Norma Pope, which is my grandmother's sister, my great aunt. I was deeply influenced by my paternal grandfather; his people came from Senegal. On my father's side, his people came from Nigeria.

My great aunt on my father's side, Norma Pope, we all agree that she was a master chef; she could cook, bake anything. You don't just call her Norma; you say her last name: *Norma Pope*.

Where does Pope come from? Was it her title or was she married?

I don't know where Pope comes from. Back in the day, I think she was married, but she never had any kids, so she helped raise my father and his siblings when his mother died—you know, my grandmother.

A lot of my family believe that I get some of my cooking gifts from Norma Pope and that part of the family. For some reason, I don't know, I was always drawn to the kitchen. I would just like to see how stuff was being done, you know?

I remember, don't know how old I was, but I would look at my mother's mother cook. I would just observe her, not asking questions. I was so short, I remember standing on a stool to see what she's doing. She would never communicate or talk to me, but she would say "go out to the yard and pick some thyme" or "go and pick some pepper," go fetch this, go get something. For some reason, though—I don't know—I kinda feel that she never liked me.

But my grandfather, he really expressed his love for me. I knew that he loved me, you know? He never called me by my name; he had a special whistle that is like, whenever I hear that whistle that means my grandfather is calling for me. No matter where I am at, I hear that whistle and I got to go; my grandfather is calling me, you know?

Six

For most of my life there has been one dream of my mother and that is to have a Caribbean restaurant of her own, staffed by her four loyal and hardworking daughters. In this fantasy life, she would spend all day with us being her sous-chef and her counter staff, passing down ancestral recipes of Trinidad through the hours of kitchen time together, her legacy of soul-orgasmic island cooking bestowed upon another generation. The cafe would not only be a place for us to work but also a business that could employ several relatives who could use the extra income. It would continue the legacy of foodmongering that exists within our family for generations in the islands. Food is a part of me; so also are the stories in my skin, the ones I must transmit to the page or be incomplete and unraveled. The dreams and feelings I vessel out of myself, they are a nourishment. I want to make my mama's food dreams come true, and I also have dreams of my own.

Seven

My mom has always been an employee in America, but back home her family had property, they had things. Her family were healers and abortionists and fertility doctors and all of the things that my hands and heart don't know how to do. They lived by the water and swam deep into the sea at daybreak. They were fishmongers, butchers. Calypsonians, singers, dramatists, heart-menders, ritualists.

Eight

Food is the way I know a lot of what it is to be Trinidadian and Cruzan as a Black girl in Minnesota. I think that is how a lot of immigrant kids learn "home," the home that exists in our blood but not in our experience. We don't know the lands and crops and waters of our ancestry, but it is archived in the foods that keep us alive.

Both of my parents were born on islands in the Caribbean that were worlds away from the landlocked Midwest they migrated to and where I was born. I was born on Dakota land, in the Phillips neighborhood of Minneapolis, and saw my mom make community with our neighbors and friends in the language of food.

One of her best friends, Ms. Linda, was a single mother like my mom, and was from Illinois; she would trade plates of southern Black cooking for my mama's Caribbean curries. There was a Vietnamese family across the street with whom we would do a similar food tasting exchange. The father, whose name was Sun, would make skewered pork on kabob sticks and would marinate it in some kind of lemongrass, otherworldly seasoned goodness. So good. I can still remember when the smell would come from across the street and eventually the transformative taste. There was a Native brother who liked my mama and would make bratwursts and bring chips and Shasta for all us kids to eat as well as wild rice from his reservation for my mom to make chicken wild rice soup, which she would share back with him.

Nine

My mom went to cooking school when I was four years old. She would take the bus to drop me and my younger sister, Oniika, to day care; then she would take the bus to downtown Minneapolis to attend school. In the wintertime, we were woken up in dark-

ness, faces wiped, and clothes and snowsuits put on. Our father felt some type of way about her going back to school and wasn't willing to help her with us, my mother told me when I was older. The main thing I remember from that time is loving her homework because it was always delicious and alchemical. Oniika and I would watch her make and decorate cakes and cookies. She would make foods from all over the world, and we would be her taste testers and sample things like borscht, hummus, and gingerbread.

My mother, like many other immigrant and low-income food geniuses, worked for minimum wage in kitchens that didn't deserve her. In those spaces she befriended people from all over the world and bonded over their traditional foods from home. When she worked at the Hyatt Hotel, on slow days the head chef would allow one of the kitchen staff to make stuff from their home countries. She learned mole from her Ecuadorian homie and how to work with Ethiopian herbs through friends she met in the basement kitchen of this wack-ass job.

Ten

She will watch anything about food and travel on TV or YouTube. She reads cookbooks like they are novels. She's the kind to go to a restaurant, eat a food that she loves, and try to re-create it in her own kitchen. Or to eat something she hates, send it back to the kitchen, and not order anything else, betrayed and disappointed at the cook's offense.

Eleven

So who are you? How would you describe yourself?

You know what, at sixty-three, I am still on that self-discovery journey. I thought at this age that I would know already. I would, like, know who I am. *This is who I am,* you know? I used to say

"I'm a mom, I am somebody's wife, I'm somebody's daughter," you know? Now, I don't know. I don't have one description of who I am. I guess I am on that journey of figuring out exactly who Ingrid is.

Where are you from?

I'm from the island of Trinidad and Tobago.

How would you describe the place that you're from in Trinidad and Tobago?

I don't know. Some people may describe it as, um, you know, a ghetto. But, you know, for me, it's home. It's where I come from. I grew up as a kid in Port of Spain, Laventille.

A small community. Everybody knows everybody and everybody's business. You know, growing up, people live so close that you can even be passing by people's window and tell exactly what people are cooking. You can smell the food.

I'm from an Anglican, Catholic community. Everybody is going to church on Sunday. Except for my family; maybe on Easter we'll go to church. But I went to Catholic school, and I didn't really like it. Why? Corporal punishment was okay. [She laughs hard here.] You know? And although we live on a dirt hill, a *red* clay dirt hill, your sneakers have to be white, you know, your uniform have pleats and it has to be pressed, and your shirt has to be white.

Kids would go home for lunch. People go home for lunch, not just kids, but like everybody, at around eleven, twelve o'clock, banks close, post office close.

I didn't know it [as a kid], but the steel pan was invented in my community. The guy's name is Bertie Marshall. He was one of my dad's friends, literally making the steel pan. History in the making.

Twelve

What is Trinidadian food to you? How would you describe it if an alien dropped down and wanted to know about the cuisine of your land? How would you speak to them about it?

The first thing that came to my mind is *global*, because there's like so many different cultures that make up Trinidad. The food I think is influenced by a lot of different cultures, but mainly African and East Indian. So I would say, in my opinion, it's an international cuisine. And delicious.

Is a lot of food like that for you? You don't exactly know the recipe but it's like an embodied or intuitive remembering?

I was just trying to think of how to write this recipe down for Case [her grandson, my nephew, whose middle name is Matthew] for macaroni pie. By his namesake, my grandfather Matthew.

I don't have a recipe for macaroni pie, but I know how to make it. I don't write things down. It's in my head.

I like to say I love my food; I make love to my food. I taste it as I go, I listen to the bubbling and the frying, and I know what to do. Most of all I take my time. I taste it; I'm looking at the texture of stuff to see if it's thick enough, loose enough. It's a feeling.

So your grandfather was your baking teacher?

My grandfather is the love of my life. I think about him more than I think of any man, you know? So anyway, my grandfather was a great cook and a great gardener. I used to follow him all around; when he's in the garden, gardening, I'm there with him. He would dig a hole, he would give me the seeds, and I would put a seed in the hole.

And so one day he decided to teach me how to make bread. I looked at him as he baked the bread, and it was delicious. Then maybe a week or so later I decided to make bread on my own. He was at work. I must have been maybe eleven, twelve, and decide to make bread on my own.

And the bread came out beautiful. Perfect shape, golden brown. I was so excited for my grandfather to come, so he could see the bread that I make. But anyways, once he cut into it, it was just like soft and gooey, you know?

I was expecting for him to be negative about it or throw it out and say, "Well, I can't eat this." Which would have been understandable if he had said that. But instead he told me where it went wrong. It needed more flour in the dough. So I thought the bread would have been thrown out. Which would have been acceptable to me. But then the following morning when I got up, he had sliced the bread [and] fried it, and he ate it. That made me feel so good. Because if he had thrown it out, I think I would have felt, I can't bake. So that was my first introduction into baking.

Thirteen

What do you love about food? Or maybe speak a little bit about what your food philosophy is, because I think you have a very strong food philosophy, actually.

I would say I love everything about food. I love the very dirt and earth that food comes from. I love the smell of organic dirt. I love planting, weeding, and nurturing the plant. I love harvesting it. I love drying my herbs.

I think it's just like a miracle, how you can get flour, yeast, baking powder, and water and some type of fat and make it into something, make it into bread, cake, or pie or what have you. I'm always just surprised and amazed.

I love using simple ingredients, you know, fresh ingredients. Yes, I live in Minnesota and you can't grow parts of the year. But I always have fresh lemon in my refrigerator, fresh ginger, fresh garlic. And one of my absolute favorite herbs is thyme.

I just love to cook. I was trained in cooking when I was living in Trinidad for the first fourteen years of my life, and I got my fundamental training without knowing it. Observing my grandmother, my grandfather, my aunt, you know, and by the time I got to St. Croix, I was cooking for my siblings [she is the oldest of seven]. All we used was like fresh herbs and spices. So that's still in me; that's how I still like to cook.

And I'm always trying to go back and to get that taste, you know? I'm always stretching back to get that taste. And it came with fresh everything. Fresh fish living on an island. Our grandparents raised chicken, turkey, ducks. On a Saturday evening, my grandfather [would] kill and pluck a chicken [for] Sunday dinner. So our meat was always fresh.

What do you want your daughters to know about food?

That food is medicine. That a lot of people spend a lot of money on clothes, you know, and designer clothes and designer bags and designer this and that. And spend the least amount of money on food. They want food on sale. I believe that food is truly medicine and if you eat, you know, you'll be healthy. And you wouldn't need for pharmaceutical. And I want my daughters to know, and my grandkids to know.

Don't be stingy when it comes to buying food, you know? Spend your money on food because it's medicine.

What do you want your last meal on this earth to be?

Lord, have mercy. Hmmmm. . . . It's simple. Callaloo. I love callaloo.

As I become older now, I realize how much I love callaloo. But a good callaloo, like what my great aunt in Trinidad used to cook. Maybe her Sunday dinner. For desserts, maybe coconut, her coconut, custard, pineapple, ice cream, and, uh, spice. Although I've been living in America for like about fifty years, my favorite food would probably be a Trinidad Sunday dinner. Macaroni pie, plantain, watercress, stew chicken, maybe some stew pork. That's what my aunt used to cook. Like I said, she was a master chef; everybody knows it.

They can say whatever they want to say about Norma Pope, but they can't say she can't cook. Probably just an island dish.

Although I've pretty much never met a food that I didn't like. You know, I love Italian food. I love Indian food. I love Chinese food, Thai. But I think it will be a Sunday callaloo, stewed chicken or stew meat, you know, preferably made by my great aunt.

Plantain fried or plantain boiled?
Boil.

Fourteen

To know my mom is to understand that she is a high priestess of food. It's sacred to her and the language and lens of her world.

Fifteen

How do you describe bake? You can't describe good food, really. The description happens in the mouth. But here is an attempt to explain it. Bake is a fried food, bread made by frying dough. The full name of it is fry bake. It's a thing a Trini mom in the eight- ies and nineties would make with porridge. Porridge is a magical and oaty creaminess that is made with condensed milk and bay leaf. It is divine, especially with that fry bake on a cold Minnesota morning.

In St. Croix they call fry bake johnny cake; in Jamaica they call it fried dumpling. In Phillips, south Minneapolis, the Native community makes the same thing and calls it fry bread, and my favorite way to enjoy it is when it's hooked up like a hood taco: sea- soned beef, cheese, lettuce, tomato, hot sauce. A curious culinary pleasure that's got a story of its own, I'm sure. Foods have their own diasporas and journeys and stories. We are Trinis on Dakota land in the midst of tundra and lakes, and we make our foods to taste home in our mouths. We remind ourselves of who we are and where we have been by the foods we eat.

Sixteen

How do you describe roti? Or pelau? Or callaloo? Or doubles? Shark and bake? Red beans and rice? Macaroni pie? Cucumber salad? Saltfish and bake? You can't describe it. You must make it and eat it and remind yourself of who you are.

. . . .

Junauda Petrus-Nasah is a writer, a soul sweetener, a runaway witch, and a performance artist of Black-Caribbean descent, born and working on Dakota land in Minneapolis, Minnesota. Her work centers around wildness, queerness, Black-diasporic-futurism, ancestral healing, sweetness, shimmer, and liberation. Her first YA novel, *The Stars and the Blackness Between Them*, received a Coretta Scott King Honor Award. And she really, really loves to eat and write about delicious food.

What We Hunger For has been typeset in Karmina,
a typeface created by Veronika Burian and José Scaglione.
It was released in 2007.

Book design by Wendy Holdman.